Chesh
Ghos
&
Legends

Frederick Woods

COUNTRYSIDE BOOKS
NEWBURY, BERKSHIRE

Based upon the Author's
Legends & Traditions of Cheshire
and
Further Legends and Traditions of Cheshire
Published by Shiva Publications
© Frederick Woods

COUNTRYSIDE BOOKS
3 Catherine Road
Newbury, Berkshire

ISBN 1 85306 110 7

Produced through MRM Associates Ltd., Reading
Printed in England

For Donald and Margaret

'Silver and gold have I none;
but such as I have give I thee.'

Introduction

CHESHIRE is a strange county in some ways. Its scenery ranges from the precipitous Peak District to the lush Plain; primarily a rural county, it somehow manages to have the greatest *per capita* wealth in England; it calls a sheep a hog and a cowshed a sheep-pen; its acre equals two statute acres plus one more in nine. Clearly, therefore, one can expect a rare and rich folklore.

Legends, myths, hauntings and superstitions abound, but apart from this collection there has been nothing in print on the subject for many years. I make no claim, however, that this book is totally exhaustive; some stories I have omitted for lack of interesting or individual detail, others because they are clearly not of exclusively local origin but appear generally throughout the country. It is though, I hope, the Best of Cheshire.

For the reader's convenience I have adopted a gazetteer approach, so that anyone who wishes to tour the county, book in hand, will be able to find the relevant entries quickly and easily. Also, as enforced administrative changes have stripped Cheshire of some of its best stories, I have taken as my area the old historical county.

Frederick Woods

ACTON

The Church and the Devil

AS will be seen in later pages, the Devil seems to have had it in for Cheshire churches in the old days. Whether they were especially pious, or whether he merely happened to be in the county on other business isn't recorded; but certainly there were frequent occasions when they apparently angered him beyond endurance.

Acton church was one that provoked his ire — to such an extent that he began hurling rocks at it. These can still be seen in a field half a mile away, which doesn't say a great deal for his marksmanship.

ALDERLEY EDGE

King Arthur and the Farmer

EACH country seems to have its legend about a great leader who will arise from his sleep and save his country again when it really needs him. Owen Glendower lies asleep in the Vale of Gwent, in a cave called Ogof y Ddinas; in Ireland Gearoidh Iarla waits in a cave under the Rath of Mullaghmast; and other countries cling to similar hopes regarding Charlemagne, Holger Danske, Barbarosa and Don Sebastian.

In England, no fewer than three saviours lie waiting for our hour of peril: the Duke of Monmouth (who,

5

judging by his performances alive, doesn't inspire a great deal of confidence!), King Harold and — inevitably — King Arthur.

Somewhat confusingly, King Arthur lies in at least three different places: in Cornwall, in the Eildon Hills and under Alderley Edge in Cheshire. Here, in a honeycomb of caves beneath the broodingly dominant hill, he and his knights and horses sleep, watched over by a wizard last seen, by conjecture, somewhere round about 1696.

A farmer was on his way to Macclesfield to sell a horse, when he was approached by a strange old man who offered to buy it. When the farmer refused, the old man told him he would not sell it at market and they would meet again that night to complete the deal. Much to the farmer's surprise — for it was a fine horse — no-one bought it. And on his way home he was again approached by the old man and was told to follow him. The farmer followed him patiently if nervously, and the old man took him past Seven Firs, past Stormy Point and past Saddle Boll, finally stopping against a blank rock face. He struck it with his staff and a vast door appeared. The two of them entered, and the old man instructed the farmer to take what payment he wanted from the gold lying in piles about the cave. Before he left he had the chance to see the bodies of King Arthur and his knights, together with their chargers, as they lay in suspended animation. Neither the old man nor the door in the rock face was ever seen again.

This story was apparently first told, at least in traceable form, by one Parson Shrigley, who was curate of Alderley Edge in 1753 and who died in 1776. He dated the appearance of the old man — presumably the indestructible wizard Merlin — at about eighty

6

years before his time, which would, as I've said, put the episode somewhere about 1696.

There is — naturally — a Wizard of the Edge inn.

ALTRINCHAM

The Haunted Cinema

THE Studio One cinema in Altrincham was haunted by the ghost of a young man who had hanged himself in the orchestra pit, back in the days when the building was the Hippodrome Theatre. Doors opened and closed by themselves, footsteps were heard, there were patches of severe cold, and a 'presence'. Seats in the auditorium were also constantly snapping down, which could only happen if the springs were broken; these were found to be perfectly in order. And in the projection room, the projectors switched themselves on and off, and there were occasional moans.

While it has never been determined satisfactorily, the theory is that the haunting was being done by the youngest son of the Hargreaves family of Rochdale, who used to own the theatre. His great ambition was to act, but when the family refused to countenance this, and insisted that he carried on as stage manager, he hanged himself.

BARTHOMLEY

The Lady and the Dog

SPECTRAL hounds are not uncommon in Cheshire, and one such can sometimes be seen running along the road at dusk by Barthomley rectory. Its appearance is said to be an omen of death. And in the fields near the dog's haunt, a white lady can be seen walking pensively by herself. No-one knows who she is.

BEESTON

The Castle and the Treasure

IT was called Castrum de Rupe long before the building of the medieval castle whose ruins still brood over the Cheshire plain; and, indeed, both Beeston and the neighbouring Peckforton Hill are obvious places for castles.

The medieval castle was begun in 1220 by the 6th Earl of Chester, Randle de Blundeville, who also built Dieulacres Abbey (see Poulton for his further adventures). When his son died in 1237 it was taken over as a royal stronghold and remained so for the rest of its active service, seeing its final conflict when it was besieged by Parliamentary forces during the Civil War.

The abiding legend of Beeston Castle is, of course, Richard III's treasure. The county had always been one of Richard's most loyal supporters and, probably for this reason, he selected Beeston to be the repository of a hoard of 200,000 marks; a mark was half a pound of silver, so the treasure would be worth approximately £9,500,000 at today's prices. Certain of its security he then rode forth to Bosworth Field and never returned.

To date, the treasure has not been recovered. Richard's men, on hearing of his defeat and death, hid the money in the well. So goes the legend, but if true, they were only too successful, for the 370 ft deep shaft has so far resisted all attempts at salvage. Following expeditions in 1842 and 1935, a well-equipped party tried again during the 1970s, but still failed to find anything in the nature of treasure.

Not surprisingly, perhaps, a subsidiary legend has grown up over the years that the treasure is guarded by demons, but no specific descriptions have ever been given, as far as the present writer can discover.

Beeston also boasts another less well-known legend, for nearby is a pool called Horsley's Bath, which is reputed to cure rheumatism.

BIRKENHEAD HALL

The Murdered Maid

THE young girl, newly taken on as maid to Lady Powell, was surely neat and pretty — sufficiently so, at any rate, for her to catch Sir Thomas Powell's eye. Or, possibly, for Lady Powell to believe that she had, since how much the love was real and how much it was a matter of her imagination will never now be known.

As month succeeded month, Lady Powell's rage grew until, one evening, positive in her own mind that her husband was being unfaithful to her, she pushed the young girl over the banisters, to crash on to the tiled floor below. When Sir Thomas returned home, all he found was the broken body; Lady Powell had already fled, on her way to the nearest port and lifelong sanctuary in a French convent.

Sir Thomas took the maid's corpse to his estate in Wales, where he buried her. He died a lonely, embittered, sad old man, the last of his family to own Birkenhead Hall.

The maid continued to haunt the place of her death until the Hall was demolished, and it is said that, even now, she can occasionally still be seen in that vicinity.

BOSLEY

The Haunted Stile

JOHN NADEN was hanged at Gun Hill at Bosley, near Macclesfield, in 1731 for murdering his employer Robert Brough, with the help of Brough's wife. Naden rifled the corpse's pockets to make the motive look like theft but — an elementary mistake to make — left his pocket knife behind at the scene of the crime, and had no alibi when challenged.

After his execution the gallows were dismantled and the wood used for a stile. It is said that Naden's ghost haunts the stile.

BOUGHTON

The Bloody Footprint

A MEMORIAL tablet was erected in Boughton to record a strange incident that took place in 1555.

A man called George Marsh was arrested in Bolton for preaching heresy at a time when it was far from healthy to be openly Protestant. Bloody Mary's reign still had three years to run, and more famous men than Marsh were sent to the stake, including Cranmer, Latimer, Ridley and Hooper. Marsh denied the charges when he was arraigned in Smithills Hall, but he was condemned out of hand and ordered to Chester Castle to await his death. As he was being led away, he stamped his foot so hard that blood poured out and trickled across the stones. Lifting his arms, he cursed the house, asking God to let the bloodstains stay for ever.

The stains stayed for a long time, certainly still visible in the eighteenth century, and some people used to claim that the footprint was occasionally actually wet. Shortly after the event, the stone was removed and thrown into a wood — presumably an action by the authorities intended to counteract the already potent anti-Catholic legend surrounding the stain — but immediately the nights were made hideous by a succession of blood-curdling noises. The authorities had to admit defeat and the stone was replaced.

More disturbances marked Marsh's execution, for when he was taken to the stake, one of the sheriffs, John Cowper, gathered an armed band and tried to prevent the burning by force. He and his men were beaten back and the fire was lit.

Marsh's ghost continued to haunt Smithills Hall for many years, his last recorded appearance being in 1732.

11

BRAMHALL

The Red Rider

ON New Year's Eve 1630, a rider galloped into the courtyard of Bramhall Hall. He was dressed in red from head to foot, with a red cloak flung back over his shoulders. Although he was a stranger, he was invited in, given food and wine, and shown to a guest room for the night. Next morning, the owner of the Hall, William Davenport, was found dead on the floor of his bedroom, and the unknown rider had mysteriously disappeared. But he still rides into the courtyard every New Year's Eve.

BROXTON

King James's Parlour

A DEEP stone chamber close by Broxton still holds mystery for the locals. Its popular name is King James's Parlour, given in the belief that King James I used it as a hiding-place during a battle. It was once clearly fitted with doors, for the marks are still visible showing where the hinges were fixed. Outside are two troughs cut into the stone, evidently for feeding and watering horses, each one with an iron tethering ring fitted.

Alternative theories are that it was once a torture chamber, or that it was a cache for loot stolen from neighbouring farms. It seems unlikely that it was ever used by James I during a battle, as no domestic battles were fought during his reign.

CAPESTHORNE

The Floating Island

FLOATING on Redesmere is an island made of peat. Legend, however, says that it was originally a conventionally fixed island which became loose owing to supernatural intervention.

A young knight, a member of the Capesthorne family, mistakenly believed that his betrothed was being unfaithful to him, and in a rage he swore never to look on her face again until the island moved on the water. Shortly after this vow, he fell seriously ill, and was selflessly nursed back to health by the innocent and forgiving girl. While he was convalescent, a tremendous storm tore the island from its roots and blew it across the mere. The young knight joyfully accepted the sign of the girl's virtue and — need it be said? — they lived happily ever after.

The Severed Hand

CAPESTHORNE Hall is the home of the Bromley-Davenport family and, as befits a magnificent old house, boasts several hauntings, one of them multiple. Below the family chapel is a vault, and a long silent line of spirits has been seen filing down into the vault. Apparently there is also a Lady in Grey who is not a member of the queue but separately haunts the main building. But the most horrific apparition of all occurred one winter night in 1958 when William Bromley-Davenport was awakened by his bedroom window rattling. Scrabbling at the glass, 'reaching out from nowhere' as he said, was a disembodied hand, severed at the wrist. With quite remarkable courage,

13

he promptly checked, throwing the window open when the hand disappeared. There was nothing to be seen down to the courtyard thirty feet below.

The apparition has not shown itself again, and the question remains as to whether it was a practical joke. But the height of the window and the absence of ledges seems to preclude the possibility; and, in any case, everyone strenuously denied involvement at the time.

Nevertheless, Capesthorne is a house where things seem to happen, as a well known MP found out when he visited the family. Throughout the night his bedroom door continually opened and closed *even after it had been wedged.*

CHESTER

Giants and Saints

THE ancient city of Chester has played a large part in the history of both England and Wales, being as it was the focal point of England's defensive (or offensive) system against the Welsh raiders. As might be expected, there are not a few quasi-historical legends associated with it.

One of the most venerable is that surrounding its foundation. Tradition says that it was once called Neomagus, founded by Magus, son of Somothes, son of Japhet, son of Noah — a tradition that sweepingly predates any known history in Britain! (Or, come to that, from at least a Biblical point of view, almost any country in the world!) Another slightly less fantastic tradition, dating from the fourteenth century, maintains that the city was founded by a giant called Lleon Mawr, after whom it was called Caer Lleon.

The name Chester, of course, derives from the Roman *castrum* — a camp — though it was then known as Deva.

The river Dee has also had its share in many of the legends. In the first place, it is reputed never to retain the body of a Christian, but to cast it up gently on one of its banks. In one case it so treated a holy statue.

In the tenth century, Cheshire was suffering from an extended drought, and Lady Trawst, wife of the Governor of Hawarden, prayed for rain to a statue of the Blessed Virgin Mary. While she was praying, a tremendous thunderstorm broke out, the immense rolls of thunder loosened the statue, and it fell on top of her, crushing her to death. The statue was tried for murder, found guilty, and sentenced to be hanged. However, when they found it impossible to hang a statue, they were forced to find another punishment. To burn it would have been sacrilege, so it was tied to a wooden cross and left on the banks of the Dee to drown. The current carried cross and statue to Chester where it was found and taken to St. John's. It remained there until the Reformation when it was torn down and used as a whipping block.

The river is also known for its odd currents which, among other things, have the habit of forming new fords from time to time. Cambrensis observed that this was a regular monthly occurrence and that victory could be foretold for England or Wales according to the way the river veered. Following one such occasion, Constable Sands got their name. The Constable of Chester had gone to help his lord Earl Richard when the latter was trapped by the Welsh on a pilgrimage

15

to St. Winifred's Well. At first the Constable's way was blocked by floods, but he prayed to St. Werburgh, and by her intervention new sand-bars emerged from the river, allowing him to cross safely in time to save the Earl.

The street that curves round the south and west walls of Chester Cathedral is called St. Werburgh's, a tribute to a gentle and powerful saint of the fifth century. She came, indeed, from a family of saints, taking her vows at an early age. She was still young when she was made Lady and President of Weedon, Trentham and Hanbury, in which position she ruled all the Mercian nuns.

The story of St. Werburgh and the geese is the best-known of all the legends. While she was at Weedon, the abbey was raided by flocks of wild geese, who ravaged the small-holdings and farms in the vicinity. In despair, the tenants turned to St. Werburgh for help. She summoned the geese to be punished, and they came to her, wings drooping penitently, so that her heart was touched and she forgave them. But one of the outraged tenants took it into his own hands to kill and eat one of them, and the geese returned to St. Werburgh for justice. She had the bones brought to her and restored them to life.

She died in AD 669, having expressed the wish to be buried at Hanbury. But she had died at Trentham, and those there kept her body against her wishes until a magical sleep overcame them all, so that her body could be taken back to Hanbury, where it was placed in a shrine and remained undecayed for almost two hundred years.

But in the eighth century, both Weedon and Trentham were destroyed by Danish invaders. The body fell to dust and the remains were taken to

Chester, where they were kept in a jewelled shrine. They were carried in procession in times of danger and displayed on the walls when the Welsh attacked. There is a record that, in 1180, 'a great fire, like to destroye all Chestre, by miracle, ceased when the holy shryne was borne about the town by the monks.' St. Werburgh now has a stone tomb in Chester Cathedral.

Mention has already been made of the Earls of Chester, who were immensely powerful. Cheshire, indeed, was virtually independent of the king in many ways, a state of affairs arising from the near-monopoly on salt production. One such Earl, Hugh Lupus, was sufficiently strong to extend his peace to any criminal or traitor (even against the king) who promised not to create trouble in his territory. And even for those in trouble with Lupus, there were recognised sanctuaries; Hoole and Overmarsh were two places where they could stay unmolested for a year and a day, if they could raise a hovel during the night and have the chimney smoking by dawn. The possibly ironically named King's Marsh, near Farndon, was sufficiently organised to have a boundary ditch; refugees who fled there had to build their huts without the use of pins or nails. (Building overnight seems to have been a fairly common tradition in medieval Cheshire, and it is said that Image House was built that way. It got its name from the fact that its walls are adorned with small stone figures representing sheriff's men, while other heads are on the porch and in the garden. These are late additions, made (and cursed) by a poacher who came to live in the house after returning from a period of transportation for killing a gamekeeper in the nineteenth century. The house stands on the Whitchurch road, just outside Bunbury.)

There is an odd tradition that King Harold was not,

after all, killed by an arrow through his eye at the battle of Hastings (or Senlac as it used to be called). Instead he was found unconscious among the bodies and taken to Winchester where he was cured by an oriental lady before travelling to Saxony and Denmark in a vain endeavour to find help to regain his kingdom. He then made a pilgrimage to the Holy Land, returning as an old man to England, where he built a cell at Ceswrthin in Shropshire and lived unknown for ten years.

Then one night he had a dream that he should go to Chester, which had been one of the last cities to hold out for him against the Normans, and where his apparently widowed queen had been given sanctuary. There he lived in a cell in St. John's churchyard for seven years, only at last revealing his true identity on his deathbed.

The Roman Legionary

THE George and Dragon on the Liverpool Road at Chester is built on the site of a 1,600 year old Roman cemetery, and it is haunted by a Roman legionary who has apparently never been relieved of his sentry duty. His footsteps go up and down tirelessly, passing through both the front and back walls.

There is also a belief that part of the canal bank is haunted, near Griffith's old flour mill. There, locals say, a misty, shifty, sinister form wreathes and writhes its way out of the dark water and spreads itself across the path waiting for prey.

Of course, it could just be mist!

CHURCH COPPENHALL

Bridget the Witch

BRIDGET BOSTOCK tends to be classified among the witches of Britain, but in fact she was both more and less. She had indisputable powers of healing and of casting out devils, and was visited by many people from Middlewich, Nantwich and beyond. As a spiritual healer, she achieved her results through prayer and — like Christ Himself — the use of spittle.

At the height of her powers she is said to have had as many as 160 patients a week, and her reputation was national, with letters about her being published in the illustrious *Gentleman's Magazine*. In spite of her fame, she remained all her life a humble woman, eking out a frugal living as a housekeeper, and refusing to accept any payment for her cures.

COMBERMERE ABBEY

The Suffering Girl

ONE of the best-known Cheshire ghosts is that of a little girl who was reputed to haunt Combermere Abbey and to foretell the death of one of the family. The fullest report appeared in the Victorian magazine *All the Year Round* (December 1870), as follows:

'Miss P—, niece of Lord Combermere, often stayed at the Abbey before her marriage. One

19

evening, Miss P— was alone, dressing for a very late dinner, and as she rose from her toilet glass to get some article of dress, she saw standing near her bed, a little iron one, placed out in the room away from the wall, the figure of a little girl dressed in a very quaint frock, with an odd little ruff round its neck. For some moments, Miss P— stood still and stared, wondering how this strange little creature could have entered her room.

'The full glare of the candle was upon its face, and as she stood looking at it, the child began to run round the bed in a wild distressed way, with a look of suffering in its little face. Miss P—, still more and more surprised, walked up to the bed and stretched out her hand, when the child suddenly vanished, how or where she did not see, but apparently into the floor. She went at once to Lady Combermere's room, and inquired of her to whom the little girl she had just seen in her room could belong, expressing her belief that she was supernatural, and describing her odd dress and troubled face. The ladies went down to dinner, for many guests were staying in the house. Lady Combermere thought and thought over this strange appearance. At last, she remembered that Lord Combermere had told her that one of his earliest recollections was the grief he felt at the sudden death of a little sister, of whom he was very fond, fourteen years old. The two children had been playing together in the nursery, running round and round the bed overnight. In the morning, he was told she had died in the night, and he was taken by one of the nursery maids to see her laid out on her little bed in the coved saloon.

'The sheet placed over her was removed to show

her face. The horror he felt at the first sight of death made so vivid an impression on him that in extreme old age he still recalled it. The dress and face of the child, as described by Miss P— agreed precisely with his remembrance of his sister. Both Lady Combermere and Miss P— related this to the writer.'

COPPENHALL

The Ghostly Raven

DURING the First World War, a young Coppenhall sailor called Wood was drowned at sea, and shortly afterwards his mother was found also drowned, in the horse-trough by Don Kinson's Oak. Thereafter a raven, generally believed in the vicinity to be Mrs Wood's ghost, was to be seen frequently, perched on its rim. The local grocer, however, was sceptical, and went round decrying the story to all and sundry until retribution caught up with him — and he too was found drowned in the same horse-trough.

The raven continued to haunt the area of the oak until Canon Reed, then vicar of St. Michael's, called in the Bishop of Chester, who carried out a service of exorcism. The raven has not been seen since.

CREWE

The Lyceum Theatre

THE handsome Edwardian Lyceum Theatre in Crewe boasts no fewer than three ghosts. Since it stands on the site of an old Catholic church and graveyard, it is hardly surprising that one of them should be a conscience-stricken monk who haunts the lower areas below the auditorium. Recent sightings, however, suggest that he has discovered a more congenial stamping-ground, since he has been seen (in May 1982) in the cellars of the Cheese Hall Vaults, the pub that backs on to the theatre.

The other two ghosts are both theatricals: one an old forgotten actor who usually haunts the area of the stage door, and the other a ballet dancer who hanged herself in the dressing-room.

All these spirits were exorcised in 1969, but the ceremony has apparently had no effect, since they are still seen from time to time. Indeed, one remarkable dual appearance occurred in the mid 1970s when both the actor and the dancer attended a play. They were seen by the entire cast of the production standing at the back of a box, engrossed in the drama. The row of children in the front of the box was totally oblivious of their presence, as indeed were the rest of the audience.

DAVENHAM

Ghosts Real and Fake

LEFTWICH HALL was, it was said, haunted by a spirit known as the Crowton Grey Lady. This shadowy figure was often to be seen, drifting through the rooms of the hall at random though, no matter what route she took, she always disappeared into a wall at precisely the same place. Eventually the wall was opened and a woman's skeleton was found. It was buried in Davenham churchyard, and the Grey Lady walked no more. Her identity has never been established.

Also at Davenham, on a small bridge on the path between Shipbrook and Whatcroft, was a 'ghost' of an altogether more spurious nature. Local villagers using the path at night were often terrified out of their wits by the sight of a dancing coffin, attended by an eerily glowing skeleton. It took a long time for the truth to be discovered: that particular path was one much favoured by poachers, who had organised the spectacular display simply to ensure privacy while they worked!

DELAMERE FOREST

The Healing Well

IN 1600 a leaflet called *Newes out of Cheshire* appeared in London, describing a 'newe found well' that could cure a wide variety of ailments. It was situated in

Delamere Forest, not far from the Chamber of the Forest, and came up at the foot of a holly tree. Numerous visitors were cured, some by bathing in the spring, some by drinking its water; among the conditions treated were blindness, rupture, gout, erysipelas, deafness and lameness. One William Johnson went there on 2nd August 1600, supported on crutches; he left them hanging on the holly bush and walked home unaided.

Centuries before there had been a St. Stephen's Well in the forest, but it had been blocked up during a Danish invasion and the site lost; it is possible that they were one and the same.

DISLEY

The Funeral Cortège

THE handsome acreage of Lyme Park was given to Thomas Danvers as a reward for his capture of the Constable of France at the battle of Crècy in 1346. Shortly afterwards, it became the property of the Legh family, and the second Sir Piers, son of the founder of the Lyme family, fought at Agincourt (1415), dying of his wounds in Paris after the battle. Tradition says that, but history says that he died in 1422.

Whichever was right, what is certain is that his body was brought home for burial, and that his wife Lady Joan was already dead from grief. His ghostly funeral cortège is still to be seen ascending the Knight's Low where he is buried, followed by a woman in white weeping audibly. Some versions of the legend say that this is Lady Joan, others — more maliciously — that it is his mistress Blanche, who also apparently died of grief and whose body was found in the meadow known as Lady's Grave.

This lady, whoever she may be, is seen more frequently than the cortège, both in and out of the house.

The Old Conservative

THE Conservative Club at Disley is said to be haunted by an old member who died one night sitting in his favourite chair by the side of the bar. In time his gentle apparition disturbed certain members and, by general agreement, the chair was moved to a cellar. Obligingly the ghost moved with it, and presumably still sits peacefully in his favourite chair surrounded by bric-à-brac, a long way from the bar.

The Unfillable Hole

ON 16th July 1823, a man named William Wood was attacked by robbers on the road between Disley and Whaley. His head was smashed in when it was forced deep into the ground by the sheer savagery of the attack. Two of the three outlaws escaped, but one of them, Joseph Dale, was hanged at Chester on 21st April 1824.

No grass grew again in the hollow caused by Wood's head, and the hole itself refused to be filled up. In 1859 one Alfred Fryer filled it with stones, but next morning they were scattered all round and the hole was empty again. Another person, intrigued by the story, went so far as to fill the hole with earth and stones and then stamp turf over it — but once again it rejected the attempt and threw the filling over a wide area.

DUNHAM HILL

Gallows Field

CHRISTIAN FIELD, belonging to Barrow Lane Farm, used to be known by a much less comfortable name: Gallows Field. The story of how it got that ominous title makes a fascinating little early detective story.

Before the days of organised postal deliveries, mail was carried on horseback from Chester to Warrington, the route passing close by the farm. One postman, called Peter Yoxhall, was waylaid by two footpads while carrying money from the sale of some pigs. They dragged him down from his horse and tied him up, lashing his feet inside his mailbag to immobilise him. Afterwards they beat him so severely that he died from his injuries, while the robbers disappeared with their plunder.

Unfortunately for them, they had recently had their horses shoed at the smithy at Dunham Hill, and eventually inquiries were made in that area. The smith, it transpired, had used an unusual type of chain shoe, and the tracks left by the robbers were thus clearly identifiable. They were traced to Birmingham, tried at Chester, and hanged — appropriately enough — at the very spot where they committed the murder, their bodies left hanging from the gibbet until disintegration.

ELLESMERE PORT

The Ghost at the Black Lion

A GHOST, most unusually dressed in contemporary costume, has haunted the Black Lion pub at Ellesmere Port for some time now. It first appeared, wearing a pin-stripe suit, walking with outstretched hands towards the wife of the then licensee, Mrs Olive Carson. The apparition's hair was falling casually over its left eye and it seemed friendly, but Mrs Carson screamed and the figure disappeared. Research showed that a previous owner had hanged himself in the room that was then Mrs Carson's bedroom.

A subsequent owner's dog refused to enter the room at all, but stayed crouched at the door, hackles bristling and growling suspiciously.

GATLEY

The Gatley Groaner

JIM BARROW lived at Cross Acres. He was uncouth, bad-tempered and mean — so mean, in fact, that he was notorious in the locality as a blatant adulterator, even watering his milk before sale. He was so thoroughly disliked by all and sundry that the whole parish gave a sigh of relief when he finally died.

But Jim Barrow's nuisance value was far from over. Racked by the pangs of conscience, he kept on emerging from his grave in Northenden churchyard, moaning and groaning his way up and down Carr Lane. As an old villager told the Cheshire folklorist and historian Fletcher Moss: 'When 'e deed Owd Scrat got 'im an' 'e warmt 'im, 'e did so, an' Jim mi't a bin 'eard a neets moaning "Oh dear, oh dear, wa-a-tered milk, wa-a-tered milk", till folks got plaguey feart a goin' yon road arter dark.' At times, it was said, he even broke into song, chanting an old song which included the apt lines:

> Milk and water sold I ever
> Weight or measure gave I never.

Not surprisingly the villagers, who had put up with enough from Jim Barrow during his lifetime, decided to put a final end to all his nonsense. The newly-arrived parson ('a scholar fresh from Oxford or Rome or someweers, chock-fu' o' book-larnin' ') called in a number of his colleagues from the surrounding parishes and, together with a party of interested inhabitants, they set off to the churchyard to lay the ghost once and for all.

A formal praying-down requires a minimum of seven clergymen, each with a lighted candle. One waits until the ghost is walking, and then cuts it off from its grave — rather like stopping a fox's earth. The wretched spirit is then surrounded and hemmed in. To quote the old villager again: 'One neet when th' moon wur out Owd Scrat mun a bin firin' up, for th' Groaner wur bein' fairly fettled by th' way as 'e moaned. An' aw th' folk got round 'im, an' they drew toart one another in a ring like, an' kept cumin' closer till at last they'd gotten 'im in a corner i' th' churchyard by th' yew tree, an' th' passon was on th' grave, an' 'e whips a bit of chalk out o' 'is pocket an' draws a

holy ring round 'em aw, an' aw the folks join 'ands
an' pray desprit loike, an' th' passon 'ops about an'
shouts an' bangs the book till 'e's aw o' a muck sweat.
An' 'e prayed at 'im i' Latin too, mind yo', as weel
as English, an' th' poor ghost moans an' chunners an'
gets littler an' littler till 'e fair sweals away like a sneel
that's sawted. An' at last th' devil wur druv out o' 'im,
an' 'e lets 'im abide as quiet as a mouse. 'E's now
under yon big stone near by th' passon's gate.'

So the Gatley Groaner was finally silenced, and
peace returned to the little village. For another, even
more bizarre, example of praying-down, see the entry
for Tushingham.

GAWSWORTH HALL

Ghosts and Perfume

THE lovely surroundings of Gawsworth Hall are
sometimes the scene of two apparitions and a strange
but pleasant emanation. The spirit of Mary Fitton —
one of the several possible claimants to the title of
Shakespeare's Dark lady of the Sonnets — is supposed
to walk in the courtyard and elsewhere. Nearby
Gawsworth rectory, reputed to have been the home
of Mary Fitton, is also the scene of some of her
appearances, when she takes a walk on an autumn
evening from the Old Hall to the Harrington Arms,
an inn standing on the site of the old lodge. Was she
keeping a rendezvous with a lover, one wonders?

Gawsworth's other ghost is that of an old playwright, fiddler and jester called Samuel 'Maggotty' Johnson. A considerable character in his day, he lies buried by his own request in unconsecrated ground in a spinney now known as Maggotty's Wood, justifying his choice in a set of verses carved on the tombstone. His lion-headed fiddle hangs on a wall in Gawsworth Hall.

The emanation is a pleasant one, a smell of incense, which first occurred in 1931 in a bedroom immediately above the Priest's Room. Ten years previously, a skeleton had been discovered when an old cupboard was removed. It was buried in the churchyard, but it is possible that the perfume may derive from that event. The incense seems to precede the visit of an archbishop, and one such even went out of his way to comment on the owners' thoughtfulness. Each time it has been smelled by at least four people, and it was last experienced in March 1977.

GODLEY GREEN

Hauntings Human and Animal

GODLEY GREEN, now considered part of Hyde, has a remarkable history of hauntings for such a small area. One of the old stone-built farmhouses, looking out over Matley and Hattersley, had a long-running history of mysterious happenings.

It was once owned by a farming family, the last survivor of which was an old dame whose nose and chin almost met. As so often happened in those days, stories began to attach themselves to this strange-looking old lady. In still earlier times, she would probably have been considered a witch, but in her day — the later eighteenth century — she attracted the doubtless gossip-worthy rumour that a vast treasure lay buried in or near the farm. And when her ghost began to appear after her death, wandering erratically through the farm at night, it was immediately assumed that she was looking for her treasure. Doors — even locked doors — were mysteriously and suddenly opened, other doors locked themselves. Beds were rocked violently and bedclothes snatched off the sleepers. Fire-irons, pots and pans rattled, and there was a noise like that of a floor being swept.

During the early and middle nineteenth century, these occurrences were so frequent that the occupants came to accept them and took no notice of them. But in 1880, two children who had been left alone in the house, heard a strange noise in an upstairs room and went to investigate. On opening the door to one room, they were confronted by an old rocking chair, swinging to and fro as if there were someone sitting in it. A farm labourer, frantically summoned, was too terrified of the sight to attempt to stop it, and finally the farmer's wife actually sat in it to still the movement. It was believed that the old woman had died in that chair.

Also, there was a certain part of the garden where nothing would grow, whatever was done in the way of gardening. Bones had been dug up there at some earlier time, and it is possible that they had something to do with the continued sterility of the ground.

In the early years of this century, somewhere about 1906, the then tenant's wife left home to go on an errand to Gee Cross, leaving her brother ill at home. On her return, accompanied by her mother, the evening was fine and still, with no sounds other than birdsong, and no wind. Suddenly in front of them, a high thorn hedge started to rock violently, and from behind it there appeared, from the direction of the farm, an apparently female figure dressed in white. And when, a few moments later, she reached the farm, she discovered that her brother had just died.

Another old lady also made regular appearances at Godley Green, so much so that the locals barely noticed her. Dressed in an old-fashioned cap, and with kilted-up skirt and apron, she would appear shaking the apron and making a peculiar hissing noise — conceivably chasing geese, but who knows? On one such occasion she was seen by a small group of visitors, who were accompanied by a relative of the old lady. 'Oh, it's owd Nancy reet enough,' he said with a touch of annoyance. 'Why the Devil can't she rest quiet in her grave? What does she want frightening people like that?'

One of Cheshire's many animal ghosts also appeared at Godley Green on several occasions. This spectral hound was described as being 'as big as a cow', with huge, yellow, staring eyes, lolling tongue and foaming mouth. It gave out a terrifying, sepulchral baying. It appeared suddenly one night on the road, in the early years of this century, next to a homegoing wanderer, keeping steady pace with him, always watching him unblinkingly. The man struck at it, and his hand went clean through it and was scratched by the hedge on the other side. Afterwards, he said 'It was the most hideous thing I ever saw. Its feet went pit-a-pat, pit-a-pat, with a horrible clanking noise like chains. I wouldn't meet it again for twenty pounds. I never want to see it again if I live to be a hundred!'

This is a convenient place to mention the Gabrel

Ratchets, a superstition that goes back to the days of early myth. 'Gabrel' is an old word for a corpse, and a ratchet is a hound; these death-hounds ride through the night sky, followed by a ghostly hunter, and to see them is a forewarning of death. Various interpretations have been put forward: it is the Devil riding out searching for lost souls; it is an old wicked squire, condemned to hunt his land through eternity for past misdeeds; it is Herne the Hunter with his pack. In fact, it is Odin, and the belief in the Gabrel Ratchets (or whatever their local name is) is common to all countries where Norse mythology has taken hold.

GREAT SAUGHALL

The Horned Woman

A woman of Great Saughall named Mary Davis developed two excrescences on her head, which changed when she was sixty into horns like those of a ram. She was taken to London and exhibited at Charing Cross. The horns eventually fell off, and one was displayed in the Ashmolean museum for many years. This was eventually mislaid, but a portrait of her at the age of 72 is believed to be still there.

HALE

The Black Friar

DURING the dangerous days of Henry VIII's dissolution of the monasteries, the treasure of the Prior of Birkenhead was hidden on the estate of Richard Leycester, his brother. That land now lies under Hermitage Road, Hale, but in spite of the suburban cosiness, the spirit of Richard Leycester, who died in the reign of Elizabeth I, is often seen guarding the treasure. This will be found again 'when a true Catholic Leycester is back at Hale,' when the Black Friar (Peter Leycester) will appear for the last time and indicate the exact location.

HEATON CHAPEL

A Murderer's Ghost

THE house at 412 Manchester Road, Heaton Chapel, was said to have been regularly haunted by a black figure, six feet high, with a dark pointed face and carrying a lantern. The figure is probably the restless ghost of an Irish labourer, one of the navvies working on the nearby railway in the nineteenth century, who had killed the children of a prostitute living at the house. In a similar house nearby, also commonly used by prostitutes, a pile of babies' bones was found beneath the floor when the house was demolished.

HILBRE ISLAND

The Lady's Cave

HILBRE ISLAND was originally called St. Hildeburga's Ey, the lady in question possibly having been Queen Hildburg of Cumbria. In the Middle Ages there was a church on the island, dedicated to the saint, though that was later replaced by a cell where two Benedictine monks lived and worked, probably as lighthouse-keepers; certainly there was a light on the island up to the thirteenth century.

When the legend of the Lady's Cave began, there was only one monk on the little island. One stormy day he was drawn out of his cave by some instinct to wander round the shore; if he wondered what had brought him out into the lashing rain he soon found out, for not far from his cave he came upon a young girl, lying unconscious on a shelf of rock.

He took her back to his cave and revived her. When she had recovered sufficiently to talk, she told him that she was the daughter of the Lord of Shotwick. Her story was worthy of a ballad.

She had fallen in love with a young knight, who returned her love. Her father, however, bitterly opposed any question of marriage, threatening to disinherit her and send her to a nunnery if she persisted with her unsuitable attachment. For a long time she was berated and browbeaten, but she stuck doggedly to her love. Then, with suspicious sudden-ness, her father's rage cooled, and he came to her with affection in his voice to invite her to go sailing with him.

While they were out in the boat, a storm blew up, and in the course of it, her father showed her a letter saying that her lover was dead. Appalled and distraught, she instantly threw herself overboard. And as she drifted helplessly away, she heard her father's voice, frantically shouting that the letter was untrue, a malicious forgery.

In spite of the monk's care, the young girl soon died in his cave, which is known even now as The Lady's Cave.

HOO GREEN

Dick Turpin's Alibi

DICK TURPIN turns up in a surprising lot of places, but the case of his Cheshire appearance gives the county a claim to his fastest ride. It is generally believed, of course, that Turpin did the famous London to York ride on his horse Black Bess, but in fact it had been made before he was even born, by another, less famous, highwayman called Nick Nevison. Nevison was never as popular an anti-hero as Turpin, and gradually public memory and then history transferred the rush to York on to Turpin. But if he didn't do it then, he certainly did something very similar in Cheshire, even if the distances weren't quite so impressive.

In the event, Turpin robbed and murdered a lawyer in Newbridge Hollow, near Altrincham. He then rode hell for leather to the Kilton Inn at Hoo Green, where he hit an ostler in the face with his whip and demanded to know the time — an effective way of fixing an alibi, if a touch brutal. And, as for Nick Nevison, it worked.

KELSALL

The Old Witch

ALES (Alice) Cawley lived at Kelsall in the nineteenth century, which is a little late in the day for reputable witches. She was known as The Old Witch of Kelsall apparently for the sole reason that she kept a live toad in a cup under her bed. This seems a harmless enough, if eccentric, pastime, but she was probably lucky that she didn't live a couple of centuries earlier, when she might well have finished up on the ducking stool —or worse.

KNUTSFORD

The Saga of Gentleman Higgins

ACCORDING to Thomas de Quincey, the 'most eminent surgeon by much in the north of England' was one Dr Thomas White, who died in 1776. He was a man of great scientific curiosity and, during his lifetime, brought together a considerable museum of professionally related objects, among which were a mummy and a skeleton. The story of the mummy will be found in the entry for Sale, where the doctor lived; but the story of the skeleton is best told here, for it was Knutsford that was the scene of much of the saga of Gentleman Higgins.

Edward Higgins was a man of remarkable aplomb — some might say total cold-bloodedness — who managed to live a dual life for years, mixing with the gentry on the one hand and murdering and robbing on the other.

Long before he arrived in Knutsford, he was well set on a life of crime. In 1752 he was tried at Worcester for sheep-stealing, but acquitted; two years later he was tried on two charges of house-breaking and was transported to America for seven years. Almost immediately after he landed, however, he broke into a wealthy merchant's house in Boston, stole a large sum of money, and escaped back to England on the next ship.

After a brief stay in Manchester, he arrived in Knutsford, where he set up house. In April 1757 he married a local woman of good family, called Katherine Birtles, and began to develop his strange Jekyll and Hyde existence. Described variously in parish registers as both 'yeoman' and 'gentleman', he must have had a good deal of presence and polish, for he was soon on visiting terms with such families as the Egertons; certainly he was regarded by all who met him as a worthy and upright citizen. Even his theft of Mr Egerton's snuffbox while being entertained at Oulton Park failed to arouse any suspicion.

Darkness saw him transformed into a robber and highwayman. Night after night he went out secretly after his wife had gone to bed, returning home in the early hours of the morning laden with plunder, his horse's hooves muffled in woollen socks to avoid detection.

On one occasion, while at a dance, he concocted an extempore plan to steal Lady Warburton's jewels, and followed her coach on its way back to Arley. He was accidentally spotted by the lady who recognised his figure and called out 'Good night, Mr Higgins. Why did you leave the ball so early?' His reply, unlike the question, is not recorded, but we can guess that it was smooth and disarming.

More successful, and demonstrative of his extreme coolness, was the occasion a little later when he broke into a house in Stanley Street, Chester, and entered a young girl's bedroom while she lay asleep. He opened and rifled her jewel box and turned his attention to the drawers. One of them creaked as he slid it open, half-awakening the young girl. She stirred and said sleepily, 'Oh Mary, you know how tired I am. Can't you put those things straight in the morning?' Higgins froze until he judged it safe to move, eventually getting safely away with a considerable haul.

Next day, going to meet the hounds at Knutsford, he saw the handbills offering a large reward, and took secret pleasure in discussing the crime with his friends. Afterwards, in his confession, he said, 'If that girl had risen up in her bed and seen me I should have murdered her on the spot.'

In spite of the fairly detailed documentation of his life, legend now begins to creep into the Higgins saga. The popular version of his eventual downfall centres on the robbery and double murder he undoubtedly committed in Bristol. He had heard of a wealthy woman there called Mrs Ruscombe, who was reputed to have a large treasure of Mexican coins. Higgins disappeared from Knutsford for a short while 'on business' and, following his return, the town 'and the whole neighbourhood as far as Warrington' was inundated with foreign gold coins. Nothing was known of the murder of Mrs Ruscombe and her maid, of course, for there was little in the way of a regular communication system in those days; and this is where Higgins made his fatal blunder, according to legend. The blunder was an elementary one: he talked to a neighbour about the murder as if it were common knowledge. It was far from that, however, and the neighbour became suspicious, finally reporting his conversation to the magistrates. Higgins was arrested, tried and hanged.

The truth is a little different. On his way back from Bristol he broke into a house in Gloucester, belonging to a Mr Wilson, and stole a large sum of money in cash. For this crime he was arrested in Knutsford shortly after his return (on what proof is no longer determinable) but escaped from Constables Abel Mossley and William Hill. A few months later he emerged from wherever he had been hiding and took a handsome house at French Hay, where he 'lived like a gentleman, kept a pack of dogs, a brace of hunters and associated with very respectable people in Bristol.' In 1766, though, his past life caught up with him and he was arrested for escaping from his transportation. As readers of *Great Expectations* will know, this crime normally carried an automatic death penalty (as did so much else in those days) but for some reason — possibly his high social standing in the neighbourhood — he was acquitted.

But now the eyes of authority were on him, and when he made a quick journey into Wales to burgle Lady Maud's house at West Mead, he was immediately arrested. He was tried at Carmarthen and this time sentenced to death.

Even then his coolness did not desert him. Shortly before the day of his execution, the Sheriff of Carmarthen received a reprieve for Higgins. It was, of course, a forgery, made and smuggled out by Higgins, but it was of such a high quality that it was at first accepted as genuine. Only when someone noticed that it bore a Brecon postmark as well as a London one did suspicion dawn. When Higgins was told that the execution was to proceed as scheduled, he received the news, we are told, 'with inconceivable insolence, treated the Sheriff with the most abusive language for presuming to suspect and inquire into what was so evident a truth.' Further, he declared that 'he would suffer himself to be torn to pieces before they should take him to that place of execution.' In the event he did not resist. As a contemporary news sheet reported, 'He died in a very sullen manner.'

So Higgins was hanged at Carmarthen on 7th November 1767, and in some possibly unofficial way, his skeleton came into the hands of Dr Thomas White and became a famous exhibit in his medical museum. What happened to it after Dr White's death in 1776 is not known, but possibly, along with the afore-mentioned mummy, it ended up in Owens College at Manchester as an anatomical teaching aid.

Mab's Curse

Mabel's Dole of pius fame,
From royale blood they say she came;
Poor and needie foulkes doe telle,
That Mynshull's land not one dare selle;
For 'Old Mab's Curse' on hym coold lighte
That ere should selle land, stone, or bighte;
His house shall come to povertee
Until another Mab we see;
Centuries under this globe shall rolle
Upon its axis on the pole
Ere Mynshull's house again shall thryve
For selling Mab's land, buts and style;
Such penance shall his sons long suffer,
And thank the Virgin 'tus no rouffer.
Blest be the son of all its race
Who thus 'Mab's Dole' shall replace.

Mab was Mabella de Erdeswick, who married William de Mynshulle in the reign of Edward I. At the time the Mynshulles owned large properties in the county, but by 1885 John Minshull was sadly able to write that the family no longer owned 'a single yard or brick'. Mabella had evidently disapproved of the sale of hereditary lands, and prophesied that if any were to be sold, all of it would go until another Mab came into the family.

The Mynshulle family had been centred around Knutsford and that town boasts another well-entrenched legend in the derivation of its name. The simple explanation is that it comes from 'neat's ford' — a place where cattle were driven across. But there is also a theory that the name comes from 'Canute's ford', as the place where that king crossed the river Lily on his way to fight the Scots. It is also possible that his ill-fated attempt to stop the tides took place on the same expedition, somewhere on the Wirral coast.

The Avenging Ghost

IN the eighteenth century, at Higher Town Common, an inn-keeper murdered a travelling rent collector for his money, and buried him in a nearby sand-hole. The crime was never traced to him, but on his death-bed, he confessed to the police — having been, he said, so haunted by his victim's ghost that he could not remain silent any longer. The sand-hole lay on a path he had to take frequently, and every time he went that way, he saw the rent collector coming menacingly towards him.

LEASOWE

The Singing Mermaid

AS we learn from the story of The Mermaid and the Bell (see under Rostherne) a mermaid used to go from the Mersey to Rostherne Mere every Easter Sunday, travelling by a subterranean passage. It seems possible, therefore, that unless there was a fairly dense population of mermaids in the Mersey in those days the Rostherne mermaid and the Leasowe mermaid were one and the same.

She was to be seen, at midnight on moonlit nights and at full tide, sitting on some boulders near the shore, close to Leasowe Castle, combing her hair and singing in the time-honoured mermaid fashion. And equally time-honoured was the fact that she was both irresistible and fatal to young men. One who found out the hard way was a sailor called John Robinson who, it is said, found her sitting on Black Rock, near Liverpool, as he went past in his boat. Disregarding all his mother had ever told him and falling helpless prey to her charms, he invited her on board, where they talked for a long time; and when she finally dived overboard again, she gave him a ring as a keepsake. We learn without undue surprise that he died five days later.

That story is taken from an eighteenth century chapbook, which seems to have got its geography a little wrong. Speed's 1610 map of Cheshire pinpoints Black Rock correctly as lying just off Leasowe.

Victims of a Feud

THERE is a legend that, during a long-drawn-out family feud, the leader of one faction was captured with his son and imprisoned in an oak-panelled room at Leasowe Castle. Rather than face the probable reprisals, he killed his son and then himself by smashing his head against the wall. Both the father and his son have been seen on many occasions, and strange noises have been heard on the stairs outside the room.

LONGENDALE

The Crusader's Return

SOMEWHERE round about the twelfth century, when it was fashionable to go off on a crusade, one of the Cheshire men who went to fight the Saracens was Sir Ro [Ralph] de Stavelegh of Staley Hall. Before he went, he took his wife's wedding ring and broke it in half, returning one half as a keepsake and keeping the other himself. (One meets this 'broken token' motif frequently in folk songs, but not so often in historical — or at least semi-historical — fact.)

Sir Ro was not one of the lucky ones; he didn't return laden down with booty as did so many of his colleagues. He was, in fact, captured by the Saracens and lay in prison for many years. One night, lying asleep in his cell, he dreamed of a great evil about to befall his wife and family. So vivid was this dream that when he awoke he knelt down and prayed fervently for deliverance. Then he fell asleep again and this time, when he awoke, he was lying in soft grass beside a massive rock called Roe's Stone, not far from Staley Hall. Amazed but thankful, he stood up and set off towards his home.

He passed various of his tenants and labourers on the way, but none recognised him. Only when he was at the door was he finally and tumultuously recognised — by his dog. The butler, alerted by the dog's reception of the stranger, looked more closely; and he too realised that this half-starved, tattered figure was none other than his master. After his initial welcome, Sir Ro sensed that the butler was holding something back, and pressed him for his news, even if it was bad.

It *was* bad. Following the news of his captivity and presumed death, his wife had been under sore pressure in maintaining the estate, and had been constantly harried by a neighbouring knight to marry him. She had resisted for a long time but had finally consented in despair; the wedding, in fact, was to take place later that very day.

Sir Ro took out his half of the ring, which he had managed to keep safely during his long confinement, and told the butler to take it to his mistress in a gold cup. Upstairs, the wife immediately recognised the token but schooled herself to caution. She came downstairs and asked the gaunt man about a mole somewhere on his body. He identified it correctly and, all doubt brushed aside, she fell into his arms rejoicing.

As a memorial to his miraculous return, Sir Ro afterwards set up a cross next to Roe's Stone, and the place was thereafter known as Roe Cross.

King Arthur and Sir Terrible

FOR a king so unshakeably fixed in the public image to the south-west, Arthur had a surprising number of connections with the West Midlands and the north-west of England. Indeed, the very name Lancashire is supposed to derive from 'Lancelot's Shire.'

This story dates from the time when Arthur had just won a great victory at Wigan. He was holding court at Longendale in celebration when an old lady came to him for help. Her young granddaughter had been kidnapped by Sir Terrible, who had already slain two knights-errant. Arthur accepted the task and went to arm himself, but a certain young squire pleaded for the honour, which was eventually given. The squire's challenge was accepted by Sir Terrible, who bade the young man precede him on to level ground. On the way there, however, Sir Terrible charged the squire in the back and was about to slay him when King Arthur, who had been secretly watching, rushed to the rescue. Sir Terrible was slain, his castle taken and the prisoners released. The castle and lands were given to the squire, who naturally married the granddaughter.

This is surely the only Arthurian legend in which a young knight gets all the prizes without actually having to do anything except be pushed over!

Prince Henry and the Werewolf

AS with the story of the Moston dragon, this legend is a fascinating mixture of myth and real people. It took place during the reign of Henry II, and began when local villagers appealed for help against a ravaging werewolf to the Abbot of Basingwerke. He cursed it to stay in its present form, whichever that was, and an eminent party immediately set out, including King Henry II, his son Prince Henry, the Lord of Longendale, the Baron of Ashton and many others.

While the Prince was separated from the other hunters, he was attacked by the werewolf, which was by now in an agonised state owing to the Abbot's curse. The Prince plunged his spear deep into its side and heard a human wail of pain. The werewolf broke the lance and attacked ferociously, ignoring constant knife-stabs and pulling the Prince from his horse. Bravely, the Prince tried to choke the beast, but his strength was rapidly failing when the Duke of Ashton appeared in the nick of time to slay it.

When it was cut up, the werewolf's stomach was found to contain the heads of three babies it had eaten that morning. A forester reported that he had seen the werewolf earlier in a glade, tearing its own skin 'as if it desired to throw it off.' It screamed and moaned piteously, sounding to the forester like a woman's voice. He, thinking the animal to be bewitched, had fled.

Robin Hood's Stone

IN one of the intervals between harassing the Sheriff of Nottingham, Robin Hood paid a visit to Cheshire and left his mark in more ways than one.

Shortly after his arrival, he met a youth wandering alone in a forest, bewailing his enforced separation from his loved one. Moved to compassion, Robin sent Friar Tuck to see the girl's guardian, an evil baron who set the dogs on the monk. The doughty friar, however, routed them with his quarter-staff and persuaded the baron to release the girl and agree to her marriage. There was a condition, however: Robin had to shoot three arrows from the tumulus known as The Butts and hit the Druid Stones now known as Robin Hood's Picking Rods. The task was, of course, well nigh impossible, but Robin sent two arrows close and hit the target squarely with the third. The mark is still there to be seen.

At this, the baron broke his word and set another impossible task, demanding that Robin cast down a great stone on Werneth Low into the valley below. Six of Robin's retinue tried and failed, but Robin succeeded in dislodging the massive boulder, hurling it down into the river Thame, where it came to rest close to Denton Cemetery at Hulme's Wood. It is still there, and is still known as Robin Hood's Stone.

Some say that, not to be outdone, Little John picked up a slightly smaller rock and threw it after Robin's, hitting it and breaking into smaller pieces. They lie there yet.

There is, however, another story attached to these stones. According to this version, a giant lived on the site of Arden Hall who conceived a deadly hatred for another giant who lived at Stockport and spent all his time hurling rocks at him. One of the rocks fell in the Thame and, indeed, it is possible to discern the giant's fingermarks in the stone. The folklorist Christina Hole suggests that the story later became attached to Robin Hood simply because he was a popular hero.

The Devil's Elbow

IN the valley of Etherow, there stood a castle owned by the Baron de Morland, whose daughter Geraldine fell in love with a wealthy neighbour, Sir Mottram de Mossland. Her love was reciprocated, but any chances of a happy marriage were shattered by de Morland's oath that he would 'send her to the Devil' if she ever spoke to de Mossland again. Being a high-spirited girl, she arranged to meet him again but as the lovers met, the Devil appeared in his own shape. With a mocking laugh, he bent his elbow and made to seize the girl, but Sir Mottram pulled her away in time, and they fled, searching for running water to cross.

Quickly the Devil caught up, but just as he was bending to seize them, a dazzling light appeared in the sky and a mighty voice cried 'Hold!' The Devil staggered, and when he had recovered both light and lovers were gone, the latter taken by fairies to haunt the banks of the Etherow as two white swans.

The Devil's arm had been turned to stone, bent as it was to grab them. So he broke it off and left it there in disgust. The elbow is still showing prominently over Longendale.

The Doctor and the Devil

A Longendale doctor once made a bargain with the Devil, with the usual penalty in return for the usual benefits. When the time was up, and he was summoned by the Devil, he arrived at the rendezvous on horseback. Seeing that the Devil was also on horseback, the Doctor challenged him to race for his soul. Although the soul was, by contract, already his, the Devil good-naturedly agreed and, even more good-naturedly, gave the Doctor a start. But he very soon drew level and to amuse himself began to twist the tail of the Doctor's horse. The horse looked round, saw what was happening, screamed with fear, and leaped into a nearby stream. The Devil, unable to cross running water, tried to pull back the escaping doctor by his horse's tail, which was torn out by the roots.

This story, which has certain similarities to *Tam o' Shanter*, is said to have taken place on the old Roman road that runs across part of Longendale, from Meldonra Castle to Brough in the Vale of Hope. It became known thereafter as 'The Doctor's Road'.

MACCLESFIELD

The Prophecy of a Regicide

> *My brother Harry must heir the land;*
> *My brother Frank must be at his command;*
> *While I, poor Jack, must do that*
> *Which all the world will wonder at.*

This rough quatrain is said to have been scratched on a gravestone in the churchyard at Macclesfield by the young John Bradshaw, whose name later became a focus of hatred and contempt when he led the signing of Charles I's execution warrant.

In the register of the parish church of Stockport, his record of baptism reads 'December, 1602, John, the son of Henry Bradshaw of Marple, baptised the tenth.' Against this entry a later hand has added the word 'Traitor'.

MALPAS

The King's Round

AN extended and witty pun concerning the town of Malpas is recorded by the twelfth century traveller and writer Giraldus Cambrensis. A wealthy Jew, he wrote, was riding in that vicinity with the Archdeacon of Shrewsbury — whose name was Péche — and the Dean, whose name was the superbly inapt one of Devil. On being told that the deaconry stretched from Ill Street to Malpas, the Jew commented wrily 'it will be a miracle if I ever get safe out of this country, for Sin is the Archdeacon, the Devil the Dean, the entry into the district is Ill, and the going forth mal pas.'

Another story arises ostensibly from the reign of King James I. During a visit to the area, he happened to drop into the tap-room of the Red Lion (as kings do), where he found the rector and his curate deep in conversation. Ordering drinks for all of them, he sat down and joined them. A little later the curate bought a round of drinks, but when it came to the rector's turn, he refused to buy the others a drink, instead quoting the local saying 'Higgledy piggledy, Malpas shot! Let every tub stand on its own bottom.' The king, who seems to have been remarkably well up in Cheshire sayings, retorted, 'Nay, nay — Maxfield measure, heap and thrutch' (in other words, give a good measure, be generous). But the rector stuck to his guns, so the king paid for the curate and left.

Retribution was not long in coming, for shortly afterwards the rector was summoned by his bishop and informed that the king had appointed the curate joint-rector of Malpas.

And, indeed, there was a joint living in Malpas for

many years, until the growth of the town necessitated new churches. And, as an indication that the episode really took place, the chair on which the king sat in the Red Lion was still being shown proudly to visitors in this century.

A nice little story indeed. Unfortunately, though, one thing spoils it. There were two rectors in Malpas as long ago as 1285 — long before the reign of King James I!

MARBURY HALL

The Marbury Dunne

> *'Here lie the bones of Marbury Dunne,*
> *The finest mare that ever run,*
> *Clothèd in a linen sheet,*
> *With silver hooves upon her feet.'*

The Marbury Dunne entered Cheshire folklore with an astounding run from London to Marbury between the hours of sunrise and sunset. She had been purchased by Lord Barrymore as a wedding present for his lady and he had promised that she would be in time for the ceremony. Sure enough, just as the sun was setting, the guests watched as she galloped in through the gates. Blood-stained foam flecked her lips as she was led to the well to refresh herself; but, like Black Bess, her gallant heart was too great for her body, and as she tried to take a drink she collapsed and died on the spot. The lady was heartbroken and died of grief

52

shortly after. Her dying request was that she should be buried, not in the churchyard, but beside the well where her mare had died.

In spite of her entreaties, Lord Barrymore buried her in the churchyard. A few days later he returned home after a journey to find his wife waiting for him by the well. She told him that as he had ignored her dying request, she would ride her beloved mare for ever. And now, at every sunset, it is said that one can see the Marbury Dunne and her mistress riding through the dusk.

Marbury Hall seems to have its problems with its deceased ladies. Two more female ghosts haunt its corridors: a Lady in Black, who has been identified as an old housekeeper, and a woman in eighteenth century dress, believed to be a member of the family.

One Marbury lady made her presence felt in no uncertain terms. At first she was embalmed and kept in a coffin in the entrance hall; no-one appears to know why, which for the present writer at least is the most intriguing aspect of the whole story. Not surprisingly perhaps, her ghost walked continually, and the next generation transferred her to the family vault at Great Budworth. This didn't satisfy her either, and the hauntings not only continued but were escalated to include constant bell-ringing. So she was disinterred and returned to the entrance hall. Things returned to peaceful normality after this, but for some reason the coffin (with the body still in it) was later unceremoniously dumped into Budworth Mere. (Once again, why? The imagination boggles.) The living members of the family can scarcely have been astonished when the hauntings began again, this time on an unprecedented scale. In the end they could stand the frequent apparitions no more and fished the coffin out of the mere. this time they buried it beside the wall of the house and peace finally reigned.

MARPLE

A Royal Retribution

MARPLE HALL was originally owned by the Vernon family and afterwards by the Stanleys. In 1606, however, it was ceded to the Bradshaw family — that same Bradshaw family that included the regicide John Bradshaw. At midnight — and presumably every midnight since 1649 — the headless ghost of Charles I appears to haunt the family whose name stood first of all among those who signed his death warrant.

Revenge seems to have been a recurrent motif in the history of Marple Hall, for it is also the haunting-ground of the ghost of Lady Brabyn, whose unrelenting spirit strove to fulfil her threat to frighten her brother and his heirs to death for expelling her from her own home.

And there were probably other ghosts as well, for skeletons were found in an old priest's hole: long-forgotten relics of — what? Murder, or sheer forgetfulness?

One small part of the Marple area used to be known as No Man's Land, and it was marked thus on some old maps, a small strip of land by the Goyt River, upsteam from Goyt Hall.

The story behind the name is that, some centuries

ago, a man stole some linen that was being sun-bleached outside a remote croft called Whitecroft Cottage. He was arrested and tried in Cheshire, but for some reason the costs of the trial were heavy and the Cheshire authorities were reluctant to pay them. While making some desperate researches into possible good excuses, a bright clerk discovered that the area where the linen had been stolen was actually under the authority of the Derbyshire town of Whitle. Naturally enough, the Derbyshire authorities didn't want anything to do with the expenses either, and produced equally convincing proof that the area was nothing to do with them whatsoever. After a lot of argument, the Crown eventually tired of the controversy and paid the trial costs itself, and the man was duly hanged at Lyme.

But as a result of that squabble, Marple ceased to collect taxes for that area, and it became technically unowned. In the end, of course, matters were regularised, but for a number of years, anyone in fear of arrest for debt could live in that croft in perfect safety.

MOSTON

The Moston Dragon

ROUND about the beginning of the twelfth century, Moston was terrorised by a horrifying dragon. According to a contemporary report, it had triple rows of fangs, flaming eyes, and a scaly, reptilian body. Six claws extended from each foreleg, and its tail was capable of crushing a bear. To meet this fearsome beast went forth Thomas Venables, son of Sir Thomas Venables, first cousin of William the Conqueror. After a lengthy fight, Venables managed to wound it with arrows before moving in to finish it off with his sword.

The field where the fight took place was called Dragon's Lake, and the Venables family commemorated the achievement in their coat of arms, which showed a dragon with an arrow in its eye, killing a child. The coat of arms can be seen carved on a screen in the Venables Chapel of Middlewich church.

MOTTRAM

The Curse of Sir John Lovel

> *'The cat, the rat and Lovel the dog*
> *Rule all England under a hog.'*

THIS famous rhyme is well-known as a political squib of its day. The cat was Catesby, the rat was Lord Ratcliffe of Ordsall Hall, and the hog was Richard III, who had a boar's head as his crest. The king and his three favourites formed a hated inner circle of power, only to be ended by Richard's overthrow.

One day, while walking in his woods at Mottram, Lovel was confronted by an old hag, hobbling along on a crutch. She cursed him, prohesying for him no children and an early unheroic death.

After the battle of Bosworth, where Lovel fought alongside his king, he fled to Flanders, but returned as a supporter of the pretender Lambert Simnel and fought in the battle of Stoke in 1487. Again he was on the losing side, and was last seen in full flight, swimming his horse across a river and gaining the far bank. Some say that he was slain in battle, though his body was never found, while others say that he fled to Minster Lovell in Oxfordshire.

With pursuers hot on his trail, and totally friendless, he dared not trust even his servants, but crept into the house quietly at night. He hid in a small secret chamber, but the door jammed and he was unable to open it from inside.

In the eighteenth century, workmen repairing the building broke into the chamber accidentally. They found a skeleton sitting at a table, its hand resting on a bundle of papers. But before they could recover from their surprise, the fresh air crumbled both the skeleton and the papers to dust.

The Changeling of Gallow's Clough

IN the seventeenth century, near to the village of Mottram, above the road to Staleybridge, a man was hanged for stealing deer. His wife had begged the steward of the estate, from which the deer had been stolen, for clemency, but in vain. So she stood sobbing by the gallows, clutching her baby during the execution; even afterwards she stayed by the swinging body to keep away the scavenging crows. Shortly after the hanging a witch appeared, intent on robbing the body of its fat, a much-prized ingredient in spells. For some reason, the witch and the young widow took to each other, and kept each other company during the long vigil, in the course of which the baby died.

A few days later, the body of the steward's baby was

found in the local woods, its face eaten away by rats. Or so the steward was led to believe.

The steward's child — for of course it was the criminal's baby that had been found — grew up, looked after by the widow and her strange friend. When he was old enough and strong enough, he became an outlaw, preying especially on the property of the steward. Until one day he was betrayed to the steward by the witch. Angrily, the steward arrested the young man and summarily hanged him. At the gallow's foot were the widow and the witch, laughing strangely throughout the proceedings.

And when the young man was dead, they told the steward it was his own son. Horrified, the man collapsed instantly. The young woman exultantly took poison, and the witch was never seen again.

NANTWICH

A Gathering of Ghosts

NANTWICH has several ghosts dotted about it, of varying degrees of trustworthiness. There is a well-documented Tudor gentleman who appears from time to time in the upper floors of Churche's Mansion, but so far — perhaps fortunately — he has not disturbed the diners in the excellent restaurant downstairs.

The magnificent Tudor Crown Hotel has also had its recent haunting. In 1978, when the area behind the hotel was being prepared for the construction of a new road, something was apparently disturbed, either by noise or vibrations, and began banging and knocking in protest. What or who it was will never be known, for a service of exorcism was promptly held, and the manifestations ceased.

There is also a reputed ghost in the parish church, though, as far as can be discovered, it has never been seen in full view, only out of the corner of the eye. There is, however, in the vicinity of the sightings, a clear window which throws an uninterrupted beam of light across the floor. Far be it from me to decry a good ghost, particularly one on hallowed ground, but it would seem as if this particular one is merely an optical illusion caused by something flicking across the path of light as it enters the building.

There are, however, odd things about Nantwich parish church. One is the abundance of representations of Jack-in-the-Green, a primitive fertility figure also called The Green Man. He appears in wood, stone and glass throughout the church, though why so many versions of a pagan symbol should appear in a Christian building remains a mystery, as do the black magic symbols carved in stone.

The present church, however, has earlier buildings beneath it. Traces have recently been found of a Norman church, but below that level it has been discovered that the church is built over running water — so much so that a pump is kept below the nave for use whenever it rains. The connection with running water seems to be clearly Druidic, and it is more than possible that, if there was a strong Druidic cult in Nantwich prior to the Christian era — or even in its early days — the Green Men may represent a continuing belief among the craftsmen and artisans of the town.

NESTON

The Restless Priest

A strange event occurred in the Catholic church at Neston, towards the end of the last century. During temporary absences of the priest, the keys were in the charge of a woman called Teresa Higginson, who died in 1905. On one occasion when the priest was away, she was approached by a strange priest who signalled to her that he wished to say Mass. He remained silent and, although she had never seen him before, he seemed to know his way around, so she made the necessary preparations for him.

When he had said Mass, he entered the vestry, followed a few minutes later by Mrs Higginson. To her astonishment, the vestry was empty, the vestments were stowed neatly away in their accustomed place, and there was not the slightest sign of the priest.

Because the affair was so puzzling, the village priest informed his bishop, who recognised Mrs Higginson's description as being of a former incumbent, now long dead and buried in the churchyard.

NORTHENDEN

The Undersized Coffin

A bizarre little tale has been collected and handed down by the folklorist and historian Fletcher Moss, one-time vicar of Didsbury. It concerns an undertaker called Bailey who was apparently a man of quite monumental laziness. While preparing for the funeral of a man with the good old Cheshire name of Legh, he built the coffin after only a quick eye-measure of the corpse. Not altogether surprisingly, it turned out to be several inches too short so, rather than go to the trouble and expense of making another one, Bailey simply cut off the head and stuck it between the corpse's legs.

There are — or were — a pair of rather sad ghosts at Northenden as well, reputed to be the shades of Sir Gaulter and a lady friend. Often at night, and especially during storms, their figures were to be seen moving restlessly beneath a yew tree that stands close to the point where the old Northen [Northenden] Ferry crossed the Mersey. Did they die in the course of running away together, possibly drowned in a sudden squall while on the ramshackle ferry? No-one knows, nor even knows whether the ghosts still haunt the spot.

OTTERSPOOL

The Murdered Cavalier

THE banks of the river Goyt at Otterspool are haunted by the unhappy spirit of John Bradshaw's daughter. Bradshaw himself was a leading Cromwellian — he was chairman of the council that condemned Charles I to death — but his daughter fell in love with a young Royalist officer who bravely visited Marple Hall while acting as courier for the king. One of the Bradshaw family discovered the affair, ambushed the young officer while he was fording the river, and drowned him there. The girl, it is believed, still mourns his cruel death.

OVER

The Prophet Robert Nixon

A great deal of confusion and ambiguity surrounds the strange figure of Robert Nixon, Cheshire's own prophet. He was born, according to one report, the son of John or Jonathon Nixon, who leased a farm called either Bank Farm or Bridgehouse Farm near Newchurch in the parish of Over. Another report, however, says he was born at Bridge End House in 1461. He was christened in 1467 — not impossible, as christenings were often left late in those days — and left in the care of his elder brother.

Nixon was, it appears, almost an idiot. An eighteenth century biography — no mention of him appears in print before 1714 — describes him as 'a short squab fellow, had a great head, and goggle eyes;...he used to drivel [dribble] as he spoke, which was very rarely, and was extremely surly...He had a very good stomach; and the report was, that he would eat up a shoulder of mutton at a meal, if they would let him, and have a good luncheon of bread and cheese after it.'

Nixon was employed as a ploughman and proved a difficult employee, given to standing in trances in the fields. In one such, at the time of the battle of Bosworth, he stopped the team of horses and stared into the distance. He cried 'Now Richard! Now Harry!' several times — and then, finally, 'Now, Harry, get over that ditch and you gain the day.' A remarkable achievement, to be sure, though the story is somewhat spoiled by the unlikelihood of his being engaged in ploughing at the time of Bosworth, which took place in August!

While working as a ploughman, the monks of Vale Royal annoyed him by their behaviour. Nixon, it is said, extemporised the rhyme:

> 'When you the harrow comes on nigh
> Soon a raven's nest will be.'

This was a meaningless jingle at the time, but it proved to be truly prophetic, for the last abbot was called Harrow. He was executed by Henry VIII, and the lands given to Sir Thomas Colcroft — whose crest was a raven. Nixon also prophesied that Norton and Vale Royal Abbeys would meet in Acton Bridge, which they eventually did, their stones being used to build the bridge after the dissolution of the monasteries.

In time, the sayings of Robert Nixon reached King Edward IV, who sent for him to come to London. But even before the messenger arrived with the summons, Nixon stated that he must go to London and there be 'clammed' [starved], a prophecy that came only too true.

On his arrival, the king decided to test Nixon and hid a valuable diamond ring. When he was asked to find it, Nixon wasn't fooled for a moment: 'He who hideth can find,' he said. The king, duly impressed, ordered that all Nixon's prophecies be put in writing, and gave him the freedom of the palace, especially the kitchen where, to the fury of the staff, he spent hours eating and drinking.

One day, however, the king departed on a hunting trip. Nixon ran after him, pleading that he should not be left alone or he would never be seen alive again, he would be starved. This can partly be explained by his well-grounded fear that, in the absence of the king, the kitchen staff would take due revenge for all his past liberties. Impressed against his will, the king ordered an officer to look after Nixon twenty-four hours a day. All went tolerably well — though Nixon was mercilessly mocked by the kitchen staff — until the king summoned the officer. Believing he would not be long, the officer locked Nixon in a closet to protect him from the staff and left hurriedly. The king kept him longer than was anticipated and by the time the officer returned three days later Nixon was dead.

Another version of this story — equally anonymous and unverifiable — places the event in the reign of James I, whose cooks, infuriated by Nixon's interminable picking at dishes in the kitchen, locked him in a closet as a punishment. The king, departing suddenly from Hampton Court to London, forgot about him.

However, how Nixon managed to do a long-distance commentary on Bosworth *and* serve King James is a bit of a mystery!

During his short life, Nixon is reputed to have correctly foretold a surprising number of events including the Civil War and the winning side, the death of Charles I and the Restoration of Charles II, the abdication of James II, the French Revolution and the war with France, the Great Fire and Plague, and the accession of William of Orange. A couple of examples suffice to give the general tone of his predictions.

On the death of Charles I:

> *'If the favourite of a king shall be slain,*
> *The master's head shall be cleft in twain.'*

The reference to the favourite is clearly to either Strafford or the Duke of Buckingham.

On the Civil War:

> *'Great wars and a pressing of soldiers*
> *But at last clubs and clouted shoes shall carry the day.'*

And another on the Civil War:

> *'Slaughter shall rage to such a degree*
> *And infants left by those that are slain*
> *That damsels shall with fear and glee*
> *Cry ''Mother, Mother, here's a man.''*
> *But after this shall be happy days*
> *A new set of people with virtuous manners*
> *Shall live in peace.*
> *But the wall of Vale Royal next the pond shall be the*
> *   token of its truth*
> *For it shall fall.*
> *If it fall downwards*
> *Then shall the church be sunk for ever,*
> *But if it falls upwards against a hill*
> *Then shall the church and honest men still live.*
> *Under this wall shall be found the bones of a*
> *   British king.'*

The wall fell upwards on 4th August 1688, at about eleven in the morning, the day being bright and clear and without the least breath of wind. Beneath the ruins of the wall were found the bones of a man of exceptional height.

There are a few memoirs of Robert Nixon, mostly dating from the eighteenth century. Some present the prophecies in verse form, others in prose. Contradictions and inconsistencies abound, as I have indicated. Nevertheless, Nixon existed and if he worked on a smaller canvas than Nostradamus he also had a remarkable run of successful predictions. It is, of course, highly suspect that no predictions were published until well after the relevant events, so that the extent of editorial contribution is unknown. Whatever the actual truth, Nixon remains a strange and fascinating character with at least a grain of truth to him. Certainly he has as much truth as the much-altered text of an old ballad, and as much validity.

The Church, the Devil and the Monks

BY tradition, Over church originally stood in the middle of the town. The Devil — who seems to have it in for Cheshire churches — picked it up one day and flew away with it. But the monks of Vale Royal pealed their bells, startling the Devil into dropping the church which, thanks to the power of the bells and the monks' prayers, fell unharmed on its present site.

> 'As Satan struggled on in pain
> His boasted strength began to wane,
> Stunned by monks' prayers and pealing noise,
> In vain he strives the weight to poise;
> Swift from his grasp it fell.'

From Egerton Leigh: *The Legend of Over Church*

POULTON

The Devil and Randle de Blundeville

IN the days when the Welsh raided regularly across the border, the monks of Poulton were in sore danger of attack. The Earl of Chester, Randle de Blundeville (the founder of Beeston Castle), had a vision of his grandfather, who instructed him to move the monks to a place of safety. Before setting off on a pilgrimage to the Holy Land, therefore, he moved them all to Dieulacres in Staffordshire.

Years later, when the Earl lay dying, a hermit still living on Poulton had a vision of a long procession passing through the night. When he inquired of their leader who they were, he was told that they were demons going to bear witness against the Earl, and the souls of his victims. The hermit saw them again on their return journey and was told that the Earl had died and his soul handed over to Hell.

The dogs of Dieulacres began baying, and bayed so long and so loud that they infected the dogs in all the other monasteries around. So great was the din that the Devil himself was forced to reject the Earl's soul. The prayers offered by Dieulacres — even in canine form — had released so many souls from eternal torment that the Devil refused to have his greatest enemy in Hell.

RAINOW

The Mysterious Footprint

ON 24th December 1735, John Turner was returning to his home in Saltersford through a heavy blizzard. When he failed to arrive, a search party was sent out to look for him. After searching for a long time, his pack horses were eventually discovered, cold but safe, but Turner himself was later found frozen to death about a mile from home. Beside him in the otherwise unmarked snow was the clear single footprint of a woman.

But whose? And how?

ROSTHERNE

The Mermaid and the Bell

ONCE upon a time, so the story goes, there was a vast tract of water stretching from Alderley to High Legh; Rostherne Mere was part of it. Every year, at dawn on Easter Sunday, a mermaid would appear, having used a subterranean passage from the river Mersey, and ring a sunken bell, afterwards sitting on it and singing (though how people could see or hear her doing that underwater is a bit of a mystery!)

The bell came from Rostherne church many years before. When the peal was being rung, the heaviest of the bells broke away and rolled to the water's edge. Three times the workmen brought it back and three times it returned to the water. Losing his patience, one of the workmen cursed it — and the bell immediately sank from sight for ever.

A not dissimilar story — though with more frightening elements — is the story surrounding the bells of Combermere Abbey, now hung in Wrenbury church. The bells were being ferried across the water, on their way to be hung, when one of them fell overboard. The man in charge of the ferry cursed it. The next minute a horrifying figure rose from the depths and dragged both him and the bell down, never to be seen again.

Possibly the monster was the delightfully named Jenny Greenteeth (clearly a relation of Fungus the Bogeyman!) who used to haunt stagnant pools covered with green slime and feed on children. Jenny's Lancashire counterpart was a little cleaner, inhabiting rivers rather than scummy pools.

SALE

Lady Beswick's Mummy

IN the story about Gentleman Higgins, I mentioned that the redoubtable Dr Thomas White had among his exhibits a mummy, and its story is bizarre in the extreme. For this was not an Egyptian mummy, but a genuine eighteenth century Cheshire mummy.

One of Dr White's regular patients was a Lady Beswick who, reading between the lines, must have been an awkward, cantankerous old lady indeed; certainly she was hypochondriac to a degree. She also had a morbid fear of premature burial. In her will, she named Dr White as her chief beneficiary, leaving him a sum reputed to be as much as £25,000 (an enormous amount in those days) on condition that he had her embalmed and kept above ground for a hundred years. A further condition was that once a year Dr White, accompanied by two witnesses, should inspect her to make sure she was still dead.

The strangeness of this was at once compounded by Dr White's own actions. After she had been duly embalmed 'by the best techniques of Paris and London', he put her in the case of a glass-fronted grandfather clock, hanging a strip of white velvet across the glass. Then, as if that wasn't odd enough, he apparently put the clock out on his roof. Thomas de Quincey was taken up to view the unusual coffin, and 'gazed upon it with inexpressible awe', as well he might have done.

So the preserved remains of Lady Beswick stayed up on Dr White's roof, regularly and solemnly inspected for signs of life once every year. Under the terms of the doctor's will, she was then bequeathed to a medical colleague, Dr Ollier, who likewise faithfully checked the corpse annually. After his death, the mummy went to the Manchester Natural History Society, where it was on view for many years until it was handed over to the Trustees of Owens College in Manchester, who finally gave the remains proper Christian burial on 22nd July 1868.

So, in the end, the old lady had her way; she stayed above ground for well over the hundred years she had stipulated. Even she must have been satisfied that the burial was not premature.

SANDBACH

The Crosses

THE origins of the famous Crosses at Sandbach are shrouded in mystery, and no-one is likely now to separate fact from fiction.

The generally accepted story — or at least the generally told story — is that during the seventh century, Peada, son of the King of Mercia, fell in love with Alchfleda, daughter of Oswi, King of Northumbria. Oswi, a recent convert to Christianity, would not agree to the marriage unless Peada also became a Christian. This Peada did, afterwards travelling to Northumbria to claim his bride. The Crosses are *said* to have been built to commemorate the return of the converted Peada and his bride (it is also said that she shortly afterwards plotted her husband's early death, so perhaps Peada would have done better if he'd stayed pagan), and the date of their erection is given, with suspicious precision, as AD 653.

They stood for a millennium, being demolished — along with so many other things of beauty and antiquity — during the Reformation, whose leaders were antagonistic to statuary as being, in their minds, close to idolatry. The Crosses carried carved scenes from the life of Christ, and were therefore broken up. The middle section of the largest went to Utkinton, where the figure of Christ on the Cross was deridingly daubed with clay. Then it went to Tarporley rectory, and thence to Oulton Park.

In 1816, the Crosses were pieced together and restored, under the direction of the historian and antiquary G. Ormerod. The fragments were widely scattered: some were found buried in the market place,

71

others were being used as paving stones, while one was being used as the step of a cottage.

A local writer called William Smith claimed to have found a verse engraved on one of the Crosses — a verse only to be read, apparently, if the reader is held head downwards over it.

> *In Sandbach, in the Sandy Ford,*
> *Lieth the ninth part of Dublin's hord,*
> *Nine to, or Nine fro,*
> *Take me down, or else I fall.*

No satisfactory interpretation has yet been made. The Crosses continue to stand in Sandbach, considerably battered now but still guarding their secret with enigmatic success.

SPURSTOW

Dead Man's Lane

IN an old issue of *Cheshire Life* published shortly after the Second World War, Beatrice Tunstall mentions an old lady who was nearly a hundred years old, whose mother had also lived to be a centenarian. And, remarkably, her great aunt had also achieved three figures, and had been in service at Spurstow Hall about 1680! Down that incredibly brief human chain, spanning such a long period, comes the great-aunt's memory of often hearing the spectral sound of 'a great dog crunching bones.' Miss Tunstall also wrote, using the same source, 'No rich pedlar left the house alive. He was disposed of, and buried beneath the pantry floor. Rich relations were imprisoned in two blind chambers, with a keg of brandy, and starved to death.'

The Spurstow family faded out as wealthy landowners towards the end of the seventeenth century, which is probably just as well if that was a fair sample of their behaviour. One of the last of the line, clearly no better than his predecessors, met a macabre and well-deserved death at the hands of one of the local farmers.

Cattle had been disappearing from the various Spurstow farms for a long time, and neither cattle nor culprit had been found. One night, however, a young man went to visit his loved one, whose father owned Haycroft, one of the larger farms on the Spurstow lands. While standing in the garden, waiting for her to appear, he heard voices on the other side of the high wall. Curious, he climbed silently up into a yew tree to eavesdrop and, to his horror, he heard three men plotting to murder the farmer and kidnap the daughter. He recognised the voices as belonging to Squire Spurstow and his two brothers. The young man dropped out of the tree and ran to warn the farmer.

On the night the attack was planned, the farmer, Adam Sandbach, was ready and waiting. The would-be robbers broke a hole in the wall, and the squire himself put his head cautiously through to check if the way was clear. His caution was well-founded but insufficient. Adam Sandbach brought his axe down on the man's neck, severing the head from the body. Outside the wall, as the body tumbled back, one of the brothers cried 'Thou has killed a better man than thyself.' 'Not an honester,' Adam retorted. 'Throw us back his head,' they called, but he refused.

73

Sandbach had the trunk carried down to the malt house by the hall gates, where it lay until next night; until relatively recently the bloodstains could still be seen on the stone floor. The following night it was carried to Bunbury churchyard and secretly buried. The route the body took on its last journey became known as Dead Man's Lane, and is inevitably haunted by the headless squire.

STANNEY

The Headless Duck

CHESHIRE is rich in ghostly animals, but surely none is more endearing — not to say eccentric — than Stanney's duck, which appeared in a lane outside the village and pecked at passing ankles. Attempts by the village parson to exorcise the duck by conventional methods failed miserably — presumably because the duck didn't know it was being exorcised — and finally, in desperation, the village butcher took matters into his own hands. Arming himself with his cleaver, he lay in wait for the duck and managed to behead it, burying the head in the ditch at the top of Stoak Lane.

Leaving aside the question of how you behead an intangible bird, it sadly has to be recorded that the butcher was only half-successful: thereafter the lane was still haunted — but by a headless duck!

(I think one final embroidery is needed for this delightful little story: surely the duck should now be carrying its head beneath its wing?)

STOAK

The Church and the Devil

FOR a peaceful county, Cheshire certainly seems to have been a constant — if unwelcoming — host to the Devil. The church at Stoak, it is said, was moved to its present site by the Devil, who for some reason objected to its original site (Ince had the same problem with fairies!). Presumably this took place between its completion and its consecration, since after consecration it should have been safe from his meddling. (But see Over church in this respect.)

STOCKPORT

The Disintegrating Man

A horrifying apparition occurred at 15 Wirral Crescent, Gorsey Bank, when a young girl was alone in the house looking after a small baby. During the evening she heard it crying and went to investigate. Coming towards her was a tall man with his arms outstretched to seize her. 'Lumps of flesh were hanging off him,' was the girl's later vivid description. In her extreme terror, she jumped through the first-floor window and broke both her legs in the garden below.

Apparently — and happily — this particular spectre does not seem to have re-appeared.

TABLEY

The Doomed Guests

AN angry duel during a revel at Tabley Old Hall resulted in two sudden deaths. One of the guests challenged another man, who he believed was flirting with his wife. The husband was killed in front of his wife, who immediately killed herself. Rather than let the scandal get out, the other guests were sworn to secrecy by the host, and the bodies were carried to a small room, which was then sealed.

Since then, the man and his wife have been seen on the gallery of the great hall, leaning on the balustrade and looking down, as if watching the dancers at a ball on the floor below.

TARVIN

The Headless Woman

GRACE TRIGG was a servant at Hockenhull Hall in the days of the Civil War. The family was staunchly Royalist and when the Hall was captured by Cromwellian troops, all the staff were interrogated in an effort to discover where the family treasure had been hidden. Grace Trigg remained steadfast even under torture and eventually the troops gave up in disgust, striking her head off with a sword to encourage the others. She is said to have carried her head to where the pub now stands that bears her name — The Headless Woman.

THURSTASTON HALL

The Distressed Lady

WHILE staying at Thurstaston Hall in the nineteenth century, an artist friend of the family who then owned the house was atonished to see an old lady enter his room. She appeared to be in great distress and stood by his bed wringing her hands. When he asked if he could help, she went across to the bell-rope, pulled it and disappeared. On subsequent nights he saw the same apparition several times, and made a sketch of the old lady. Although the current owner of the Hall knew of no ghosts, when the artist showed the sketch to a previous owner, it was immediately recognised as an ancestress, whose portrait once hung in the Hall.

TILSTONE FEARNALL

The Giant Monk

AT Tilstone Fearnall, there is a dip in the main Nantwich-Chester road at the end of Rookery Lane, which is known as 'Haunted Hollow'. The story arises from a bizarre happening during the last century, when two girls, accompanied by a dog, were suddenly confronted by a cowled monk that they afterwards described as being 'about ten feet tall.' The spectre advanced slowly down the lane towards the girls and passed right through them. The dog fled hysterically, followed by the two terrified girls. Their brother, C.R.

Bell, hastily harnessed a horse to a governess's cart and went out to investigate. There was nothing to be seen, though the horse reared unexpectedly several times at the corner where the monk had appeared. Subsequent investigation discovered that the figure had been frequently seen.

It is relevant to add that a Saxon abbey had been in existence close by, which is mentioned in the Domesday Book. A later Benedictine abbey was founded on the same site in 1093 by Hugh Lupus and dissolved in 1540.

TUSHINGHAM

The Ghost in the Bottle

I had thought that only Cheshire could boast a ghost duck; but it is even odder than that. It actually boasts *two* ghost ducks!

The Blue Bell Inn at Tushingham once had a pet duck. Doubtless it started out as a cute, fluffy little thing adored by all and sundry, but it grew up to be distinctly misanthropic. Of course, this is understandable enough: no self-respecting duck would relish a life of being accidentally kicked in a crowded bar, having ale splashed over it, and probably being half-choked by clouds of tobacco smoke into the bargain. In the end it rebelled and turned to pecking at so many intruding ankles that it was at last reluctantly killed by the landlord. However, he was apparently sufficiently soft-hearted not to eat an erstwhile family pet;

instead the duck was interred beneath the bottom step of the stairs going down to the cellar.

That should have been the end of the story, but the duck clearly hadn't yet had all the revenge it wanted. Regularly thereafter, the step would come loose, no matter how firmly down it was nailed, and the duck would emerge, to reappear upstairs, pecking away to its heart's content.

In the end, the landlord turned to the church, and the local parson arranged a praying-down ceremony. As we have already seen, seven parsons are the minimum required for a praying-down, but this parson was nothing if not thorough and, with an enthusiasm that can only be described as overkill for one little duck, rounded up no fewer than twelve. Things didn't go quite according to plan, though, for instead of returning to its grave under the stairs, the duck remained where it was. But gradually it started to shrink. With a sudden flash of genius, the local parson waited until the wretched bird was small enough, and then shoved it into an empty bottle, hastily jamming the cork tightly in. The bottle was bricked up in a wall, and peace returned once again to the Blue Bell.

More recently, when the pub was undergoing repairs, the bottle was carefully removed from its hole, and later sealed back into the new wall. Clearly even today no-one was taking any chances.

UTKINTON

The Gambling Mare

UTKINTON HALL is supposed to have been built round a living tree. Its owners, the Done family, were Puritans, frugal people who shunned worldly amusements of all kinds.

Two traditions have attached themselves to the house. The first is the charming belief that all the blackbirds in the walled garden are the descendants of a ghost in the form of a bird exorcised by a priest. The other is of a different kind entirely, and concerns Irish labourers who had been employed to build some stables. Either the Dones' ban on worldly entertainment did not extend to their employees, or the labourers were merely ignoring instructions, but the story goes that they were playing cards in the stable one Saturday night. So engrossed were they that they did not notice the chiming of midnight. A moment later, however, it was drawn forcibly to their attention when an old mare turned round in its stall and inquired whether it might join the game. The labourers, understandably enough, fled and never returned.

VALE ROYAL

The Enchanted Abbey

WHEN the young Edward I was returning home from a crusade to be by his father's deathbed, a storm sprang up which threatened his ship. Edward vowed that, if his life was spared, he would build a monastery for Cistercian monks in Cheshire. Immediately the sea became calm, and the ship made harbour, only to sink suddenly and mysteriously in port after all had gone ashore.

The place chosen by Edward was called Queterne Hallows. The woods round the abbey glowed with an unearthly light, and heavenly music was heard by all who visited it, both during the work of building and after completion. The bells rang at midnight by themselves.

Robert Nixon (see Over) prophesied that this proud abbey would become a raven's nest, and this came true in Henry VIII's day, when the building became the property of Sir Thomas Colcroft, whose crest was a raven.

WHALEY BRIDGE

The Skull of Tunstead Farm

TUNSTEAD FARM possessed a skull, believed to have belonged to a young girl who was murdered there. The front part was entirely missing, and there was a hole in the back, said to have been caused by the fatal blow. Many strange events were connected with this skull over a long period, especially when a member of the family was about to die, or when strangers came to the farm, whether they were merely new farmworkers or intruders. Strange and frightening noises were heard at night when any sort of emergency impended.

Once a ghost appeared to one of the tenants, a Mr Lomas, while he was sitting in the kitchen keeping watch over a dangerously ill child in the cradle. At one point in the evening he became aware of a young girl bent over the cradle but, assuming she was a maid, dismissed her, saying that he could look after the child. The maid vanished, and the child died shortly afterwards.

Mr Lomas was also often warned about a farm crisis by a tapping on the window whenever a cow was about to calve or when he was urgently needed in the lambing season.

At one point in the farm's history the skull was buried. Although the burial took place on consecrated ground, the noises increased drastically, until the tenants were forced to return the skull to its normal resting place in the house. On another occasion it was stolen and taken to Disley, but it set up so much noise and disturbance that the thieves hastily returned it. These manifestations occurred at the farm and Disley simultaneously.

WINWICK

The Ghostly Pig

BOTH the site and the name of Winwick church were determined by a supernatural pig. During the first night of the building, the pig was seen at the site crying 'Wee-eewick'. Throughout the night, it carried the stones one by one to a place nearby where St. Oswald,

King of Northumbria, was killed in AD 642. The founder of the church took this as a divine sign, accepted the new site, and later had a belled pig carved in the tower above the west entrance. However, pigs are supposed to be sacred to St. Antony. Following the death of a lord in the streets of Paris, from his horse stumbling over a pig, all pigs were banished from the streets except those belonging to the monastery of St. Antony, provided they wore bells. The Cheshire scholar Egerton Leigh also provides another explanation: in consequence of the gratitude of pig owners to St. Antony for miraculously eliminating all pig diseases, a belled pig was kept at the expense of the parish.

WIRRAL

The Last of the Masseys

THE Masseys were one of the leading Cheshire land-owning families and, in their time, considerable patrons of the arts. Indeed, it is believed that the unknown author of *Sir Gawain and the Green Knight* may have worked for them. Certainly the long poem is written in a dialect that could have come from Cheshire, Lancashire or Staffordshire, and much of the poem's action takes place in the county.

All the iles of Anglesey on lyft half he
  holdes
And fares over the fordes by the forlondes,
Over at the Holy Hede, til he had eft bonk
In the wyldernesse of Wyrale.

(Holy Hede is probably Holywell, a centre of pilgrimage where St. Winifred had her head cut off and miraculously restored — an event closely paralleled in *Gawain*.)

The last of the Massey family was William, who made the mistake of being a Jacobite, fighting for the invading Scots at the battle of Preston in 1715. He managed to escape from the carnage, forcing his horse on and on in a panic-stricken, headlong gallop. In spite of the animal's exhaustion, he swam it across the Mersey and got safe home to Puddington where, like Black Bess, it collapsed and died. Knowing that a search would be made, he attempted to establish an alibi by beating a passing countryman not far from home, hoping to prove (in another parallel with Dick Turpin) that he couldn't possibly have been at the battle. Unfortunately for him, the plan went sour on him when the man sued him for assault. The alibi was broken and Massey was immediately arrested. He was sent to Chester Castle to await his trial, but froze to death in his cell before the court could meet.

CHESHIRE DIALECT

IT should come as no surprise that a county so rich in tradition and folklore should also be rich in colourful dialect words. Most of these have almost entirely dropped out of common use, a sad loss which is yet another result of uniform broadcast English and State education. Rather than such verbal wealth should be forgotten, I append a short list for enjoyment and — hopefully — for revival.

Those who wish to study this aspect of Cheshire folklore more closely should consult Egerton Leigh's *Dialect of Cheshire* (1877).

Ackerspyre	To sprout
Addle, yeddle	To earn
Agged	Tired
Aimer Gate	Short cut
Algerining	Prowling about with intent to rob (derived from the Algerian pirates)
All macks	All sorts
Allegar skrikers	Thin gruel with vinegar flavouring
Aneend	Upright (in the sense of not lying down)
Antiprunty	Restive (used of a horse)
Arsemart	Knot grass
Asker	Lizard
Athurtens	The other side of
Audfarant	Old-fashioned
Awming	Standing and staring
Axings	Banns of marriage
Badger	Dealer in corn
Baggs	Commercial traveller. In past days, he went on horseback, carrying his goods in saddlebags. He was also known as a KCB — Knight of the Carpet Bag.
Bain	Near, convenient
Balks	Hayloft
Bandy hewitt	An ill-favoured dog
Bangbeggar	A beadle

Bangle	To waste
Batter dock	Butterbur
Bawson	Badger (the animal)
Bawtert	Clogged
Bearbine	Woodbine
Bedeet	Dirty
Bells	Fuchsia
Biggening	Recovery of women after childbirth
Bing	To begin to turn sour
Birds' eggs	The haw
Birr	Impetus (to take birr — to run hard)
Bittlin	Milk bowl
Black Jack	Black beetle
Blart	To low like a cow. (Just as 'shippen' — cowshed — derives from 'sheep-pen', so this clearly derives from 'bleat'. Strange lot, Cheshire farmers!)
Bloaten, bloatch	To be very fond of
Blood wall	Wallflower
Blue buttons	Devil's bit scabious
Bobberous	Pert, saucy
Boose	Cow-stall
Boots yellow	Marsh marigold. Also called mayflower.
Bor tree	The elder
Bracco	Diligent
Braggett	Spiced ale
Bridneeze	Bird's nest
Brizz	Gadfly
Bullhead	Tadpole
Burr	Sweetbread
Cammed	Crooked
Cample	To scold
Cank	To gossip
Cankum	A prank
Caperlash	Abusive language
Capo, capel	Working horse
Cassartly	Risky, uncertain
Caukum	Practical joke
Churl's treacle	Garlic
Cloggy	Compact, neat
Clussumed	Clumsy
Cobbst	Unruly, fractious (of children)
Cobnobble	To chastise
Cocam	Sense, judgment

Cocket	Pert, saucy
Collywest	The contrary
Cotquean	Man who interferes in women's work, especially in the kitchen
Cowshat	Wood pigeon
Cradant, cradantly	A coward, cowardly
Cramble	To hobble
Cranny	Agreeable
Cratch	Manger
Creachy	Out of order, in bad repair
Crewdle	To crouch
Crow orchard	Rookery
Crumpsy	Bad-tempered
Cuckoo's bread and cheese	Wood sorrel. Also known as cuckoo meat
Cumberlin	Annoying person
Dacity	Intelligence, quickness
Daker hen	Corncrake
Davely, deavely	Lonely, retired
Deaf	A nut without a kernel is said to be deaf
Deg	To sprinkle
Degging can	Watering can
Demath	A day's math or mowing for one man, generally used for a half-acre. (Not, however, a Cheshire acre which in true Cheshire fashion isn't an acre. It is, in fact, two statute acres and one more in nine. Nine Cheshire acres would therefore be nineteen statute acres. Is that clear?)
Devil's parsley	Wild chervil
Dodder	Convolvulus, or any straggling plant
Dogeous	Soaking wet
Dree	Disagreeable
Dreven	Draggletail
Dumberdash	Heavy rainstorm
Dunch	Deaf
Dungow-dash	Dung
Durcratch	Side of a cart
Eamby	Close by
Eating water	Drinking water, as distinct from *Carry Water*, which is water with an excess of iron chalybeate, fit only for swilling.
Edther bowt	Dragonfly

Eggs and butter	Buttercup
Eshin, eshintle	Pail, pailful
Fac	Soil
Fairies' tables	White rot
Farantly	Orderly, clean
Fashous	Shameful. From the French 'fâcheux'
Fastens	Shrove Tuesday
Feaberry	Gooseberry
Fearcrow	Scarecrow
Festerment	Annoyance, sometimes confusion
Filmart	Polecat
First end	Beginning
Flaskers	Bewildered
Fleck	A flea, or to catch fleas. Also, confusingly, the fur of a rabbit or hare. Flough is also a flea.
Flurch	Large quantity
Foo-gawd	Bauble, toy
Forkin Robin	Earwig
Foxy	Wet, marshy
Fremd	Strange, hostile
Fridge	To rub to pieces
Fudge and fash	Nonsense
Fugle	To whistle
Fummuz	To meddle
Fuzziky	Spongy
Gafty	Doubtful
Gammock	To fool around
Gawin	To understand
Geen	Clever, active
Getty (pron. jetty)	To agree, to get on
Gib and gill	Male and female ferret
Gilhooter, hillhooter	An owl
Glead	A kite (the bird)
Gleads	Embers
Globed to	Foolishly fond of
Glottened	Astonished
Gomeral	Idiot, soft-head
Gorby	Soft, silly
Gorse hopper	Whinchat
Graft	Depth of a spade
Graith	Riches
Grash	Fruit

Grosier	Gooseberry
Ground Ivvens	Catsmint
Grumell	Rubbish
Guttit	Shrovetide (*ie* Good Tide)
Haffle	To hesitate
Hailow	Shy, bashful
Harbouration	Collection
Hattle	Wild, skittish
Hattock	A hole in the roof where owls nest
Headaches	The poppy
Heart-rooted	Said of a tree that is self-sown
Heazy	Hoarse
Hebbon	Worth having
Heckle-tempered	Short-tempered
Herb Peter	Cowslip
Herbive	Forget-me-not
Hoynd	To make a bad bargain
(By) Hulch and stulch	By hook or by crook
Hullet	Owl
Hurch	Touchy
Hurry	A quarrel
Imbrangled	Entangled
Incle	Tape
Insense ·	To instruct
Insett	Household
Jack Nicker	Goldfinch
Jack Sharp	Stickleback
Jannock	Upright, honest
Jow	To bang
Kazardly	Accident prone
Kecksy	Hollow
Kedlock	Charlock
Kench	Sprain, strain
Knacketty, Knicky-knacky	Adroit
Knobs	Lavender
Ladies' smock	Cuckoo flower
Lake, lakin	To play, plaything
Lambs' ears	Rose campion

Lancashire gloves	Hands without gloves
Large Dicky Daisy	Chrysanthemum
Lathe	To ask, invite
Leath	Leisure
Leazecaster	Old name for Chester
Leet, leeten	To pretend
Licksome	Pleasant and agreeable
Lite	A little, a small quantity
Litigious	Used of bad weather that stops harvest work
Loffeling	Idling
Lommer	To climb or scramble
Lullies	Kidneys
Lungeous	Violent
Lurkey dish	Pennyroyal
Madpash	A madman
Mafflement	Concealment
Mag	To chatter or scold (from 'magpie')
Meg Harry	Tomboy
Merricking	Rollicking, fooling around
Meterly	Moderate
Mislest	To meddle
Mixon	Midden
Mizzick, mizzicky	A bog, boggy
Mizzle	Light, misty rain; also to run away
Moggins	Clogs
Moondark	Money secretly saved by a wife
Mortacious	Very
Mosey	Overripe
Mouzle	To mess, make untidy
Muckinder	Dirty handkerchief
Muggin (to receive a)	To be beaten up. As they say, there's nothing new under the sun!
Mulligrubs (to have)	To be in a bad temper
Mulsh	Drizzling weather
Naked virgins	Autumn crocus
Nattered	Ill-tempered
Neezle	To nestle
Nizzly	Drizzling
Nomony	A tale, yarn
Nookshotten	Crooked, disappointed
Nosrow	Shrew (the animal)
Nurring	Active, clever

Obshackled	Limping, lame
Old man	Asthma, but also the herb southernwood or Lad's Love
Ownder	The afternoon
Pad	Path
Paigle	Primrose
Pash	Puddle
Pillgarlic	A valueless object
Pingle	Small croft or field
Plim	Perpendicular (plumb)
Poler	Barber
Poot	Pullet
Pottle	Measure of two quarts
Pouk	Pimple
Powfagged	Exhausted
Powsels and thrums	Dirty scraps and rags
Punger, pungow	To bother, to puzzle
Puthery	Hot and close (of weather)
Quank	Quiet
Queen's feather	London Pride
Queeze	Wood pigeon
Quirken	To choke
Racconals	Oxslips
Rache	To smoke (of a chimney or fire)
Raddle	To beat
Radgy	Ill-tempered
Rakussing	Noisy, boisterous
Rase-brained	Impetuous
Razzored	Angry
Red rag	The poplar
Reef	Skin rash
Rigatt	Small channel made by rain
Rigg	Strong blast of wind
Rip	To speak vehemently
Rittling	Runt. Also 'ruckling'.
Robinrunith hedge	Bindweed
Rog, rogging	To shake, shaking
Root	To meddle
Rosamund	Wild garlic
Rotten	Rats (plural of 'rot')
Rute	To bellow, roar

San Jam Pear	The Green Chiswell pear, usually ripe about 25 July, St. James' Day. Altrincham used to have a Sanjam Fair on that day.
Sand pot	Quicksand
Scaffling	Eel
Scharn	Cowdung
Scranny	Thin, meagre
Scrat	Hermaphrodite
Scoperil	Rascal (used affectionately)
Scouver	Scurry, confusion
Scrapedaystions	A miser
Scurrick	Scrap, particle
Scutch	Couch grass
Seneve	A corpse when it begins to change is said to seneve. So is a joiner's work when it warps.
Shackussing	Shambling
Shakassing	Idle
Shandry	Farmer's gig
Shattery	Harebrained, giddy
Shedom	Surprising, strange
Shepstir	Starling, from the fact that the bird hunts for insects on the animal's back and stirs it up.
Shim	Clear bright light
Short-waisted	Short-tempered
Shutting	Harvest home
Sibbed to	Related to
Sitten	Burned
Skellerd	Crooked
Skew-wifter	Something that is out of shape
Skitterwit	Scatterbrain
Skrike	To shriek. Hence 'skrike of day' — cock crow.
Skuds	Owl pellets
Slancing	Prying
Slattery	Of wet weather
Sleck	To extinguish, to slake
Slive	To cut off, divide
Slood	Rut
Sloven	Divided (past participle of 'slive')
Slurr	To slide
Sluther	Muck, dung
Smastray	Garden warbler
Snudge	A sponger

Soldiers	Red campion
Songal, songow	Gleaned corn
Soss	A heavy fall
Sowl	A plough
Sowring	Vinegar
Spact	Mentally quick
Springow	Nimble, active
Sproze	To boast
Staggering Bob	Newly-born calf
Steady	Anvil
Stinking Nancy	Scabious
Strout	To swell out
Suck	Ploughshare
Swaddledidaff	A sweetheart
Swag	To warp
Swippo	Nimble. Also the thick part of a flail.
Tank	A blow
(To) Tarr on	To excite to anger
Teen	Anger
Terry-diddle	The bittersweet
Tether-devil	Woody nightshade
Threap	To insist
Thrutch	To squeeze
Tic	Foot and mouth disease
Tine	To lose one's temper
Titback	Horseback
Titmaups	Titmouse
Tom and Jerry	A public house
Tooty pot	A hole in the road, usually full of water
Trashert	Poorly shod
Tummuz	Toad
Tungled	Plagued
Tupp cat	Tom cat
Twarly	Peevish, cross
Twiggery	Osier bed
Twist	Appetite
Twitch clog	Black beetle
Twothry	A few (two or three)
Upceck	To upset
Urr	To growl, snarl
Varging	Quarrelling

Wall	Spring of water
Walm	To boil
Wammocky	Weak, feeble
Wangle	To totter
Warrabee	Wart
Waunt	A mole
Wayberry	Plantain. Also known as 'Wibrow worrow'.
Whabble, whabbock	Puddle
Whany	A blow
Whave, whoave	To overhang, to arch
Wheady	Measuring more than it appears to do
Wheam	Convenient, near
Wheamow	Nimble
Whiskettle	Basket
Whistle bally vengeance	Bad, poor quality beer; diluted swipes
White Nancy	Narcissus
Whooked	Ill, shocked
Wimblé	Gimlet
Windering	Diminishing
Withering	Strong
Wooan, wone	To dwell
Wording hook	Dung fork
Work brattle	The will to work
Wychen, wickey	Mountain ash. The tree was believed to be a specific against witches.
Yaff	To bark
Yarly	Early
Yewking	Having a sickly appearance
Yobbins	Outcries, yells. Used in the plural only.